THE

Home Mortgage

Book

Insider Information Your Banker & Broker Don't Want You to Know

By Dale Mayer

Withdrawn From Montgomery-Floyd Regional Library

THE HOME MORTGAGE BOOK: INSIDER INFORMATION YOUR BANKER & BROKER DON'T WANT YOU TO KNOW

Copyright © 2007 by Atlantic Publishing Group, Inc.
1405 SW 6th Ave. • Ocala, Florida 34471 • 800-814-1132 • 352-622-1875–Fax
Web site: www.atlantic-pub.com • E-mail: sales@atlantic-pub.com
SAN Number: 268-1250

No part of this publication may be reproduced, stored in a retrieval system, or transmitted in any form or by any means, electronic, mechanical, photocopying, recording, scanning, or otherwise, except as permitted under Section 107 or 108 of the 1976 United States Copyright Act, without the prior written permission of the Publisher. Requests to the Publisher for permission should be sent to Atlantic Publishing Group, Inc., 1405 SW 6th Ave., Ocala, Florida 34471.

ISBN-13: 978-0-910627-84-9   ISBN-10: 0-910627-84-3

Library of Congress Cataloging-in-Publication Data

Mayer, Dale, 1961-
  The home mortgage book : insider information your banker & broker don't want you to know / by Dale Mayer.
     p. cm.
  Includes bibliographical references.
  ISBN-13: 978-0-910627-84-9
  ISBN-10: 0-910627-84-3
  1. Mortgage loans--United States. 2. House buying--United States. I. Title.

  HG2040.5.U5M39 2008
  332.7'220973--dc22
                              2007050619

LIMIT OF LIABILITY/DISCLAIMER OF WARRANTY: The publisher and the author make no representations or warranties with respect to the accuracy or completeness of the contents of this work and specifically disclaim all warranties, including without limitation warranties of fitness for a particular purpose. No warranty may be created or extended by sales or promotional materials. The advice and strategies contained herein may not be suitable for every situation. This work is sold with the understanding that the publisher is not engaged in rendering legal, accounting, or other professional services. If professional assistance is required, the services of a competent professional should be sought. Neither the publisher nor the author shall be liable for damages arising herefrom. The fact that an organization or Web site is referred to in this work as a citation and/or a potential source of further information does not mean that the author or the publisher endorses the information the organization or Web site may provide or recommendations it may make. Further, readers should be aware that Internet Web sites listed in this work may have changed or disappeared between when this work was written and when it is read.

INTERIOR LAYOUT DESIGN: Vickie Taylor • vtaylor@atlantic-pub.com

Printed in the United States

Printed on Recycled Paper

We recently lost our beloved pet "Bear," who was not only our best and dearest friend but also the "Vice President of Sunshine" here at Atlantic Publishing. He did not receive a salary but worked tirelessly 24 hours a day to please his parents. Bear was a rescue dog that turned around and showered myself, my wife Sherri, his grandparents Jean, Bob and Nancy and every person and animal he met (maybe not rabbits) with friendship and love. He made a lot of people smile every day.

We wanted you to know that a portion of the profits of this book will be donated to The Humane Society of the United States.

–Douglas & Sherri Brown

THE HUMANE SOCIETY
OF THE UNITED STATES ©

The human-animal bond is as old as human history. We cherish our animal companions for their unconditional affection and acceptance. We feel a thrill when we glimpse wild creatures in their natural habitat or in our own backyard.

Unfortunately, the human-animal bond has at times been weakened. Humans have exploited some animal species to the point of extinction.

The Humane Society of the United States makes a difference in the lives of animals here at home and worldwide. The HSUS is dedicated to creating a world where our relationship with animals is guided by compassion. We seek a truly humane society in which animals are respected for their intrinsic value, and where the human-animal bond is strong.

Want to help animals? We have plenty of suggestions. Adopt a pet from a local shelter, join The Humane Society and be a part of our work to help companion animals and wildlife. You will be funding our educational, legislative, investigative and outreach projects in the U.S. and across the globe.

Or perhaps you'd like to make a memorial donation in honor of a pet, friend or relative? You can through our Kindred Spirits program. And if you'd like to contribute in a more structured way, our Planned Giving Office has suggestions about estate planning, annuities, and even gifts of stock that avoid capital gains taxes.

Maybe you have land that you would like to preserve as a lasting habitat for wildlife. Our Wildlife Land Trust can help you. Perhaps the land you want to share is a backyard—that's enough. Our Urban Wildlife Sanctuary Program will show you how to create a habitat for your wild neighbors.

So you see, it's easy to help animals. And The HSUS is here to help.

The Humane Society of the United States
2100 L Street NW
Washington, DC 20037
202-452-1100
www.hsus.org

TABLE OF CONTENTS

SECTION 4: YOUR PERSONAL MORTGAGE ANALYSIS.............. 169

CHAPTER 14: ORGANIZATION OF INFORMATION 171

CHAPTER 15: ANALYZE & CHOOSE YOUR MORTGAGE OPTIONS 181

SECTION 5: YOUR PERSONAL MORTGAGE JOURNEY.............. 185

CHAPTER 16: THE APPLICATION PROCESS 187

CHAPTER 17: NEGOTIATING THE PERFECT HOUSE 189

INTRODUCTION

Finding and securing the best mortgage for the purchase of your dream home can be a confusing and daunting experience. Even people who are not actively shopping for a new house are often inundated with mortgage offers, and with all the different options to choose from, you will want to ensure that you are getting the best loan and rate for your particular circumstances.

Buying a new home can be an ominous process, whether it is your first home or your tenth. Many home buyers are overwhelmed, even frightened, by the financial aspects of a home purchase, but finding the perfect mortgage loan at the best rate for you does not have to be a difficult task. The best defense you have against feeling overwhelmed is staying informed. Reading this book will help you obtain the necessary information, and the mortgage process will soon become understandable, making you more confident and capable as you approach your home purchase.

You will learn how to find the best mortgage opportunities from among the many that are out there. You will learn how to negotiate with lenders, how to get the type of mortgage loan that is most appropriate for your needs, how to calculate how much you can afford to spend on a new-home purchase, how to understand the true cost of a mortgage and evaluate your capacity to repay the loan, how to prequalify for a mortgage, how to understand the lending process from inception to completion, and how to analyze the various mortgage products that are available to you.

You will also achieve a better understanding of what you want in a new house versus what you need, an important distinction that escapes many new home buyers. You will gain knowledge regarding financing, budgets, and credit reports and credit scores. The authors will provide you with the information you need to create an appropriate home-buying schedule for your situation. You will also learn about the process of building a new house, purchasing an existing home, and the advantages and disadvantages of manufactured homes.

The authors will discuss setting home values; explain home warranties, homeowner's insurance, closings, inspections; and much more. You will learn about creative financing options, buying with little or no money down, how to uncover hidden assets that can increase your worth, and how to enhance less-than-perfect credit.

This comprehensive resource contains a wealth of modern tips and strategies for financing and closing on your house. In addition to traditional resources for securing a mortgage, you will learn about researching and securing a loan on the Internet, where it is possible to discover outstanding mortgage options that might not be available through conventional lending channels. You will also find out about government programs that, if you qualify, can assist you in the purchase of your new home. Even though you might feel you are relatively cash-poor, or you have a less-than-perfect credit rating, you can find the house you have always wanted and acquire a favorable mortgage for its purchase.

SECTION

1

PRELIMINARY CONSIDERATIONS

The main purpose of this book is to equip the reader with enough information to find the perfect mortgage. However, you will not need a mortgage until you find the house you want to buy, so some preliminary considerations regarding home purchases should be covered at the outset.

You will need to know how to begin searching for a new home, what you should be looking for, and how much house you can afford based on your personal financial situation. As with any other goal, a home purchase is best approached by beginning with a carefully constructed plan. The first, most basic element in your plan for a home purchase should be a determination of your house-related wants, needs, and budget requirements, all of which are likely to be intertwined with other aspects of your life. In this section of the book, we will look in depth at the decisions you will need to make and the requirements you will have to meet before beginning your search for a new home.

In **Chapter 1,** we examine your wants for your new home, your needs in a house, and the difference between the two, as well as your capacity to repay a mortgage based on your financial situation and credit rating.

In **Chapter 2,** we discuss the importance of location in your search for a house, as well as real estate appraisal options and suggestions for creating a personal home-buying schedule.

In **Chapter 3,** we introduce your options for a home, including the purchase of an existing tract home, the construction of a new home, and manufactured home options. When you are finished with this book, you will be well equipped to choose the best mortgage for you.

Good luck and congratulations. This book is a good first investment toward affordable home ownership.

USE YOUR INPUT & LOGIC IN CREATING A PLAN

In your purchase of a new home, you will conduct a good deal of research, receive advice from diverse sources, and be inundated with information. No matter how much your real estate agent and lender try to influence your decisions, the decisions about every aspect of your home purchase, from the type and location of your new house to the type and terms of a mortgage, are yours alone. Knowing this will allow you to approach the process with confidence, and when your purchase is complete and you have moved into your new home, you will feel that the outcome is in your best interest.

You must begin this endeavor with a plan. The plan need not be so detailed that it accounts for everything from the color of the carpet in your new bedroom to the material used in the counters of your dream kitchen. Your plan just needs to be a guide that you can refer to during your home search that will continually remind you what you are trying to accomplish so that you can avoid temptations and last-minute influences.

Whatever your reason for embarking on the journey to homeownership, this book will guide you toward the best decision you can make for your circumstances. Buying a home is, for most people, the biggest and most expensive investment they will make. Do not take this process lightly, but be sure to enjoy it as well, so that you make the right decisions and are able to revel in your new home, confident in the knowledge that what you wanted and needed coincides with what you ultimately got.

The first thing you must do before starting is to decide what you need based on your life goals. To do otherwise will likely lead to issues you do not need to deal with. Only you know what your particular situation is, and while we try to deal with it as specifically as possible, you will have some decisions to make on your own.

Just because you might have been doing some research and gathering information on real estate and mortgages does not mean you must act right away. It might be too early at this time for you to buy a home, whether because you are not ready for the process, are not in a financial position to seriously consider homeownership, or consider the current real estate market to be wrong for your current situation. Sometimes the most important step in purchasing a home is the realization that the time is not ripe for a purchase.

Never lose your vigilance. Stay up on current real estate issues and continue to update your research. It is dangerous to think that simply because you have read a book or two about mortgages, you know everything that there is to know about the topic. Real estate and mortgages are complicated subjects, and no one resource can cover them completely. There will undoubtedly be issues that crop up for you that are not covered in this text; however, a combination of sources will give you fairly comprehensive information, so do your research.

Most important, trust yourself. The fact that you are willing to expend the effort to educate yourself by reading this book is proof that you are willing and able to make good homeownership choices. Now let us get started.

WANTS VERSUS NEEDS: AN IMPORTANT DISTINCTION

When you dream of your ideal home, do you envision a multimillion-dollar mansion with marble and stained glass, pools with cabanas, and state-of-the-art electronics? Maybe if you win the lottery or start pulling down an immense salary, this type of house will be an attainable option in the future. Unfortunately, the average home buyer's wealth forces them to make some potentially difficult choices. You must approach a home purchase with an acceptance of what you can realistically afford, which means ultimately deciding between which aspects of your desired home are truly needs and which are simply wants.

Most first-time home buyers want to buy the biggest house they can possibly afford for the lowest possible price. Many people think this approach guarantees maximization of the return on their investment. However, this mind-set can cause big trouble for you and your finances.

Think it through. If you buy the biggest house that your real estate broker can find for you based on the maximum loan your mortgage lender says you are eligible for, you might also be buying a massive headache each month when your mortgage payment is due. Your finances might change, your income might go up or down, and other debts might creep up, but you will still be required to make your mortgage payment, and a big house costing the maximum amount of the mortgage for which you qualify amounts to a huge payment over the lifetime of the loan. You might have to cut back on things that you previously enjoyed to make this huge payment; more problematically, you might find you cannot make ends meet and have to cut back on expenses in other necessary aspects of your life, such as food, gas, tuition payments, health insurance, and other essentials.

Beware, for you might end up cursing the day you bought such an expensive house. After a few months of struggling to meet your mortgage payments, you might realize that you did not need an enormous walk-in closet in each bedroom of the house, or that the colossal basement prewired for a home theater is not being used since you cannot afford to install the theater.

Buyer's remorse is particularly excruciating when it is associated with a purchase as sizable as real estate, and you do not want to live in what you once thought was your dream home at the expense of your financial and emotional health.

To avoid the problems that come when you overextend yourself, it is important that before you even look at the first house on your list, you determine exactly what it is that you need. List the essential items that you require in a house, and nothing more. In creating this list, you might, for example, consider the following:

- How many bedrooms will you require? Forget about a guest room, a den, a craft room, and the like. The required number of bedrooms should be based on the number of people in your family or on your future family plans.

- Is it absolutely necessary that you have a basement? Do you have to have an enclosed garage? Why? For example, if you live in a location where some seasons are extremely hot or extremely cold, a garage might be a necessity. On the other hand, a basement might be nice, but in some parts of the country, particularly in the Southwest, the land is not conducive to excavation, so digging a subsurface level is likely to be too expensive to justify.

- How close do you need to be to work? Would a longer commute cause problems? Is public transportation a feasible option? Perhaps it is feasible for you to live further from your place of work and telecommute some of the time. Consider your flexibility, which is a crucial aspect of committing to public transportation or carpooling. Also, do not disregard how your commute might affect your mental and emotional health; even if it proves to be less expensive to buy a house that results in a longer commute to and from work, if you find it too difficult to spend the time on the road or away from your family, the distance might not be justified.

- If you have children, what schools are available for them to attend in your area? Is there a specific district that you must be in to be eligible for attendance at a particular school? Can you afford to pay tuition for a private school if you are dissatisfied with the public school in your area?

- Do you have the time, ability, and willingness to deal with a less expensive fixer-upper? Or are you unwilling or unable to provide the care required for a home that is in less-than-perfect condition and instead desire a home that you can just move into and be done with?

Undoubtedly, you can think of a number of other such questions applicable to your situation. The major goal of distinguishing between your needs and wants is to establish a baseline. This line is a fixed level, with everything that is absolutely required in your home above it; anything below the line are wants, things like that basement theater or walk-in closet that are nice perks only if you can afford them once all the necessities are taken care of. If and when you find yourself limited financially in your new-home purchase, the wants below the baseline will be the first to be crossed off the list.

Once you create this list, put it in an accessible place and come back to it often during your search. Referring to the list regularly will help you refocus on what you need in a home after you have been out looking at houses that include what might seem at first glance like needs, but that turn out to be simply wants.

THE CASE FOR RENTING

If you have searched for a home for a while and have not found a house that falls within your budget and meets all your needs, renting might be a better option, at least for a limited time. The realization that renting is a more fiscally responsible option for you shows maturity. Renting can be a practical way to build up your savings for a down payment and initial mortgage payments on a house that you love and can afford, especially if your income is limited but anticipated to increase, or when the buyer's market is high.

Before you decide that buying a house is the only thing that will satisfy you, consider the following:

- Renting allows you more flexibility in terms of geographical location than owning a home. Because the term of a rental lease is finite and much shorter than a mortgage commitment, if you decide to relocate, all you have to do is pack your things and go. Plus, living somewhere first while renting lets you get a feel for that location; you can check out your work commute, the quality of the schools, and the safety of the neighborhood before you commit to the purchase of a home there.

- When you rent, you often do not have to deal with maintenance issues or the cost if anything on the rental property goes wrong. Instead, the landlord is responsible for repairs and replacements. The costs can become an alarming homeownership surprise the first time you have to spend a thousand dollars or more on a new water heater so you can have a hot shower in the morning.

- If you rent, you do not pay property taxes, which can be significant depending on your geographical location; you also are not responsible for homeowner's insurance, another significant homeowner cost. You might be required to purchase renter's insurance (even if not required, renter's insurance is still strongly recommended), but this is considerably lower than homeowner's insurance. In addition, some of or all your utilities might be covered by your landlord in a rental.

- When the housing market is rising at a fast pace, or is out of sync with the economic reality in your area, renting allows you to avoid the risk of home values that might ultimately crash, leaving you with a mortgage that is higher than the value of your home.

Renting before purchasing a home offers you the freedom to move and insulation from the costs of homeownership. Plus, in almost all markets, average monthly rent is less than the mortgage payment on real estate of a similar caliber. By renting, you keep your costs as low as possible and take on no real estate market risk.

HOW MUCH CAN YOU AFFORD?

After you have decided what you need in a home, your next determination must be how much you can afford to spend. The easiest way to find out what you are qualified to purchase is by working with a lender who can give you a prequalification letter or get you preapproved.

PREQUALIFICATION

Prequalification is often easy to get and does not take much time. Most lenders have this process streamlined to a ten-minute consultation with some basic information plugged into a formula. Unfortunately, because of the limited information you provide in an application for prequalification, the lender is not committing to loaning you the amount that it qualifies you for. So while this process is easy, it is not terribly accurate, and you are not guaranteed anything by the lender.

PREAPPROVAL

Preapproval is different than prequalification. Preapproval almost always requires that you begin the mortgage application process with a lender. This is a much more involved scenario. You will likely need to provide documentation of your income, tax returns from the previous year, and, sometimes, verification of your monthly expenses.

Essentially, preapproval is a quicker way of applying for a mortgage. After you have been preapproved, you will have a much firmer grasp on how much you can borrow, and the chance of something going wrong with the financing is dramatically reduced because the lender is actually committing to lending you the funds they have offered in the preapproval.

STARTING THE PROCESS

The real estate agent will likely ask you almost immediately whether you have been prequalified for a loan. Agents will ask this question for a number of reasons, but the most obvious is to find out what type of property you are eligible to buy.

Agents desire prequalified customers because they know up front what these customers can afford and, more important to the agent, that if they sell a customer a house in that range, they will get a commission because financing will not be an issue. Prequalification came about because agents were not happy that they could show dozens of homes to a potential buyer and then find out after the purchase contract was signed that the buyer came nowhere near qualifying for the financing they needed.

Lenders also appreciate prequalification because they no longer need to depend on real estate agents for referrals. Lenders can advertise that they offer prequalification letters. After you obtain a letter and go through the process of finding a home within that qualification range, you will likely come to that lender for the financing. Thus, lenders now have some control in real estate financing.

If you are prequalified by one lender, you can likely be prequalified by many different lenders, so shopping around is a good idea. There are thousands of choices out there for the savvy home buyer, and you do not need to limit your options.

YOUR CREDIT SCORE

There is nothing more important in your financial life than your credit score. This number will influence nearly every decision that is ever made about your ability to apply for and receive credit. About the only thing you can do that is not directly influenced by your credit score is to make savings decisions. However, the more you must spend in interest for loans, the less you will have available to save, so your credit score indirectly affects every aspect of your financial life.

It is a good rule of thumb to know your credit score before you start looking at houses, and definitely before you meet with your lender for the first time. It is even better to pull your credit report to check for any errors or other problems.

A credit report contains information about all your credit decisions throughout your life. Everything that you have ever done to hurt your credit will be obvious on the report. The lender is going to double check the report and will find any problems.

Credit scores and reports are covered in detail in Chapter 13.

IMPROVING YOUR PURCHASING POWER AND CREDIT

You have examined your budget and discovered that you cannot afford the house of your dreams or that your credit is not stellar. Sometimes this comes as a shock, but most people in this situation suspected this was the case. There are many things you can do to turn your situation around for the better, and these steps are relatively easy if you are determined to do them.

While it might be tempting to try and find a mortgage program that will work with your current financial situation, you should think about this idea first. Are you in this situation because you cannot control your spending? If so, that is not likely to change after you own a house. And while you will be building equity by owning a home, if you cannot get a good mortgage product, you will be building equity slowly. With a few changes and a little effort, you could be in a totally different situation within a year with a much better chance of building equity more quickly and also saving a significant amount of money along the way.

If you decide to try for a mortgage that will allow you to purchase a house now, you should still implement the following tips. Otherwise, you will be in the same situation, if not worse, when you decide to move up to another house.

First, analyze your spending habits. Do you know where your money is going on a monthly basis? Chances are you have not kept a close eye on your money and most of it disappears. Consider the following:

- **How much do you spend on food?** Do you eat out a lot? This is an expensive habit, and most people do not realize how much they spend on it. If you do not want to eliminate dining out completely, you might want to split a dish at a restaurant or go to less expensive places. Maybe it would work better if you got takeout and saved on the expense of drinks and a tip. The best thing to do is to cut down significantly. Even if you do not eat out often, you might be spending a good sum of money on frozen dinners and other prepackaged items at the grocery store. The more packaging and preparation that is involved, the more expensive it is. Go to discount chains and buy your groceries with coupons. It might take a little more time and effort, but you will be able to cut your monthly food expenses significantly using these strategies.

- **Stop using credit cards.** Credit cards create financial hardship for most American consumers. Often, you will overspend with a credit card, believing that you will pay for the difference the next month. However, that rarely occurs. Plus, credit card interest is quite high and can keep you in debt longer than you think. The best thing you can do is cut up all your credit cards and cancel the accounts. Go on a completely cash-based budget. Not only will this force you to live within your means, but you will appreciate your spending more when you are paying with cold, hard cash.

- Do you really need a new car? Most Americans possess a nice, newer-model car at all times, without even thinking about it. As soon as they pay it off, and often long before they do, they upgrade to a better model. Not only does this keep you constantly in debt and making car payments, it also does not make much sense, since cars depreciate in value for every mile they are driven. There are all kinds of dependable cars with good gas mileage that cost a fraction of what you would pay for a new car. Why do you have to have a new car when a car that is close to being paid off will work just fine? If you want to save a ton of money monthly, keep the car that you have paid off. If you have an expensive new car, sell it and use the money to pay down debt and buy another, cheaper car. This is the quickest and easiest way to save a substantial amount of money monthly.

- Do not buy the newest and best clothes, furniture, or appliances. You can easily find used items that are just as good as new ones, but at a fraction of the cost. In our consumption-driven economy it is easy to go out and buy everything brand new, but you are not getting your money's worth. As soon as you buy any of these items, it instantly drops in value, sometimes by half.

There are worksheets in Chapter 14 that will help you understand where your money goes each month and assist you in establishing a clear picture of your financial state.

Your goal should be to save money, reduce debt, and repair your credit. If you do these things, you will dramatically turn around your financial situation within a year. You will have less debt and maybe even some savings for a down payment. This will be reflected in your credit score and will help you get more favorable interest rates on your mortgage. Plus, you will have developed some financially healthy habits that will allow you to continue to build wealth, and you will save a significant amount of money on your mortgage. Remember that the house is the goal. Real estate goes up in value and is a stable investment, unlike the numerous consumer goods discussed above.

WHERE & WHEN

WHAT IS IN A LOCATION?

Have you given much thought to the part of town where you would like to live? Where you situate yourself within the area will determine the real estate value of your home, as will your choices of neighbors, environments, and schools. All these issues might not be applicable to your situation, but at least one of them will be — real estate value. Your ability to borrow money for a home purchase will depend in large part on the appraised value of your home. Real estate values can fluctuate tremendously from one side of town to the other, one county to the next. There are steps you can take to fully investigate these areas before beginning your home search.

First, get to know a real estate agent who is not representing you or any property you might be interested in purchasing. You need an impartial agent who can give you objective information. Real estate agents are the most educated people when it comes to assessing property values, the impact of a particular area on real estate values, and behind-the-scenes information about certain neighborhoods, neighbors, and school districts.

While talking to a real estate agent is a good idea, there are other ways to get this information. An agent might not be unbiased, even if they know up front that you will not be using them. Talk to other people who are in the know, including real estate attorneys, appraisers, home inspectors, and local officials that assess property taxes. All these people will have an opinion about which are the best areas, which ones are growing in value, and which ones you might want to avoid. Do your homework when assessing where you might want to live; it can save you thousands of dollars, and possibly make you thousands of dollars, if you choose wisely.

To make the best decision, you need to consider several aspects of the house. The first is the location. Think about it — you can change a lot of things about a house once you own it. You can redo the kitchen, put on new siding, and add landscaping to dramatically spruce up a home. These renovations are limited only by your financial ability and, in some instances, zoning. The one thing you can never change, however, is the location of your home. If it is located in an undesirable area, that location will not change no matter what renovations you undertake. That is why many people say location is the most important aspect of your real estate purchase.

A poor location can be defined by a number of criteria and is subjective. You will want to consider:

- Whether it is located near heavy industry or any other type of noisy, smelly, or dirty enterprise.

- Whether it is in an area that is known for high crime or that is deteriorating.

- Whether the local economy is beginning to take a downturn or people are starting to leave in higher-than-usual numbers.

You should consider these factors because, while you might be able to deal with them, potential buyers down the road might not — a bad situation to be in when you want to sell. These problems will likely continue to exist for some time and will be a huge detriment to the property's value.

HOW TO FIGURE OUT THE BEST PLACE TO CALL HOME

To accomplish this step, you are going to have to make trade-offs and try to find the location that will fulfill the most priorities. First, identify the areas where you can afford a house; there is no sense looking in a neighborhood that is out of your price range. When you have identified the neighborhoods you can afford, prioritize your list of needs.

If you are young, single, and do not plan to have children, you do not need a big place and do not need to worry about schools. Your goal should be to find a place close to work and social venues such as malls and restaurants. If you are looking to get some money out of the real estate when you move, you might also consider areas that are not perfect for you right now, but are up-and-coming neighborhoods.

If you are a married couple that has or wants to have children soon, your priorities are obviously much different. The size of the home will be a prime concern; you will want to ensure that you have enough rooms to accommodate a family. You will also want to check out the schools and rate them. The distance to work and social venues might not be as big a concern in this case.

After you have identified one or two different areas, investigate further. Start exploring the neighborhood at different times of the day and on different days of the week. You might be surprised at how different these areas can be depending on the day or time. Check out the newspaper and go to open houses in the area to see what the homes are like without being pressured to buy. You might even want to walk around the neighborhoods and talk to people who live there. Most residents will be happy to share their thoughts.

Another consideration is how long you plan on being in a particular area. Many people have jobs that uproot them on a regular basis. If you are in this position, you will want to consider resale value, which will be important in getting back the money you invested in the house when you sell. You should also think about financing options that would best fit your situation. If you know that you are going to be in the house for only five or six years, there are mortgage products that you could take advantage of to save thousands of dollars in interest. There is more information about this in the mortgage section of the book.

Anyone who has already been through this process knows that there can be important considerations that pop up later. That is why it is helpful to create a customized chart of what is important for you and your new house.

This worksheet is a good place to start. Add or delete as required to prioritize the factors that matter to you. It is highly suggested that you create a worksheet for each house you are considering. As you walk through one after another, you will forget the details that made each of them unique. Even better, add columns to this worksheet and view information about three houses at once. This way, you will be able to compare the information easily.

HOME BUYER'S WORKSHEET

Address: _____

_____

Asking Price: $_____

Location:

	Yes	No
Is it near your area of employment?	☐	☐
Is it near your partner's area of employment?	☐	☐
Is it near the proper schools for your children?	☐	☐

HOME BUYER'S WORKSHEET

	Yes	No
Is it close to major shopping centers?	☐	☐
Is it close to public transportation?	☐	☐
Is it close to a freeway?	☐	☐
Is it near a religious gathering place?	☐	☐
Is it close to an airport or train station?	☐	☐
Safety Issues:		
Is it close to a hospital?	☐	☐
Is it close to your doctor, dentist, or medical clinic?		
Are there sidewalks to walk on?	☐	☐
Is it a safe place for your children to play?	☐	☐
Is it on a main street?	☐	☐
Are the streets well lit?	☐	☐
Is it in a light traffic area?	☐	☐
Is there a security system?	☐	☐
Neighborhood Value:		
Are the other properties well maintained?	☐	☐
Are the streets and alleys well maintained?	☐	☐
Are there parks or green spaces nearby?	☐	☐
Is the area zoned residential?	☐	☐
Is there construction planned for the area?	☐	☐
Are there any environmental concerns?	☐	☐
Outside the House:		
How old is the house? _____		
Are the property boundaries easily distinguishable?	☐	☐

HOME BUYER'S WORKSHEET

	Yes	No
How old is the roof? _____		
Is the property landscaped?	☐	☐
Does the house appear to be in good condition?	☐	☐
Is there a deck?	☐	☐
Is there a patio?	☐	☐
Is there a fenced yard for the kids?	☐	☐
Is there a garage?	☐	☐
Is the driveway in good condition?	☐	☐
Is there parking?	☐	☐
Is there any visible damage?	☐	☐

Describe: _____

_____

The Basics:

	Yes	No
Does the house have electric heating?	☐	☐
Does the house have oil heating?	☐	☐
Does the house have gas heating?	☐	☐
Does the house have hot-water heating?	☐	☐
Is the electric system so old it might need work?	☐	☐
Is the plumbing system so old it might need work?	☐	☐
Are there storm windows?	☐	☐
Are there screens on the windows?	☐	☐
Is there a basement?	☐	☐
Is there an attic?	☐	☐
Is the house on a sewer system?	☐	☐

HOME BUYER'S WORKSHEET

	Yes	No
Does it have a newer furnace?	☐	☐
How old is it? _____		
Does it have a newer hot-water tank?	☐	☐
How old is it? _____		
Inside the House:		
Is there an air conditioner?	☐	☐
Is there a dishwasher?	☐	☐
Are appliances included?	☐	☐
Is there a dining room?	☐	☐
Is there a washer and dryer?	☐	☐
Are there washer and dryer hookups?	☐	☐
Is there a fireplace?	☐	☐
Are the window coverings included?	☐	☐
Is there a family room?	☐	☐
Is there a separate suite?	☐	☐
Is it legal?	☐	☐
Does it have the right number of bedrooms?	☐	☐
Does it have the right number of bathrooms?	☐	☐

Special Features: _____

_____

WHEN TO BUY

There are many theories for the perfect time to purchase a home. The first thing you will want to do is watch the interest rates and know what the economy is like in the area. Home prices surged in recent years, and many people were caught up in an unrealistic real estate market that could not be sustained. These same people are now finding themselves with a house that has dropped in value significantly below the purchase price. This will not be an issue if you are aware of what is going on in your local real estate market.

Essentially, when it is the best time for you to buy, get ready to buy. Do not wait on factors that you cannot control, such as the time of year or the interest rates. If you are financially able to afford a home and are ready to take on the added responsibility and costs, do it. Do not go out and buy a house before you are ready just because the talking heads on TV or on the radio say that it is the best time to buy — doing so is a good way to get into a situation that you are not ready for financially or personally.

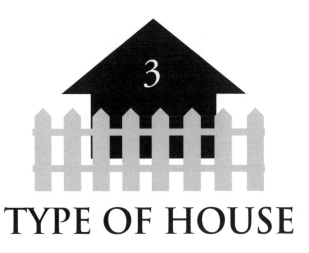

TYPE OF HOUSE

CONSTRUCTION OF A NEW HOME

Many people want to build their own house someday; it is the American dream to create a house that is truly your own. However, this concept is also an expensive and complex process. New construction costs more than buying an existing house because new homes are often larger than existing homes in the same community, and there are many one-time costs that you have to cover that subsequent owners will not have to deal with. These include sewer hookups, connecting roads, electricity, and so on. If you are not in the best financial position, you would do just as well to purchase a home that already exists.

Another issue in new-home construction is that a home might be built in an area that is not developed or established. Developers often want to buy a piece of property that is cheap and resell it for a much higher value once the city starts expanding toward it. Therefore, it is likely that not only will the development not be established, but that you will be further away from restaurants and shopping. You also might be in a poorer school district and community until the development takes off and the city builds out to it.

New construction will often grow in value faster than existing homes because the area that it is built in will continue to change and grow for some time after it is built. It will eventually hit a plateau and begin rising at about the same rate as existing homes, but you will get a kick-start of equity if the house is built well in a decently put-together development.

New construction will allow you to build the home of your dreams, and this is appealing to many people in this country. However, there are also many people who are interested in preserving the past or who might enjoy architecture that existed years ago in the community. Therefore, there are a number of people who will opt to find a fixer-upper in a good part of town that they can use to re-create history. If you are a handy person who does not mind putting in some sweat equity, this might be the route for you. Not only will you enjoy your home more when you had a major hand in re-creating it, but you can increase its value substantially by fixing up a historical home.

BUYING AN EXISTING HOME

By far the most common real estate transactions in this country are single-family, detached dwellings. These homes are often located on their own plots of land and come in a number of shapes, sizes, and conditions. If you are looking to get into a good home quickly, you will likely want to purchase an existing home.

There are always existing homes available in your area that will fulfill your needs. If you choose an existing home, you will know what kind of area it is because it will already be fairly well established. You also will likely be closer to shopping and social activities.

MANUFACTURED HOUSING

A manufactured house is a house that is built in segments in a factory and then moved to the home site, where it is affixed to the foundation and assembled. Before you balk at this option, think about it. This option offers you the chance to buy a home that will appreciate in value — albeit not nearly as well as a single-family home — for much less than the typical home. It is an opportunity for many people to get into a house and stop paying rent. You should at least consider this type of house as a way to put your money into an asset that should gain in value, so that when you move up to a site-built house, you will be able to get that money out of it in equity.

A trailer, the typical mobile home, is completely self-contained. In most cases, a mobile home is located in a mobile-home park, where the owner of the home rents the plot of land that it sits on. These are much less desirable than the more modern manufactured housing.

Manufactured homes are of much better quality than trailers, and they are usually created as a part of the lot, which the owner of the house also owns. These houses will retain their value and go up in value just like a site-built house; however, the rate of increase is nowhere near that of a traditional house. These manufactured houses should last almost as long as traditional houses and are an option for those just starting out.

SECTION

2

BESIDES THE
MORTGAGE

Although the mortgage process and the many pieces of information surrounding it might seem overwhelming, there is more to consider. Choosing a mortgage product is not the only step you will need to take. Many other issues come into play when you are examining available mortgage options and attempting to save some money in the process.

In **Chapter 4,** we will introduce you to terms such as purchase agreement and home warranties, discuss if and when to hire an attorney, and whether any possible home inspections must be performed.

In **Chapter 5,** we will discuss escrow and its relationship to the mortgage, private mortgage insurance, and homestead options for property taxes.

In **Chapter 6,** we will talk about the down payment, including common types of down payment and how the amount of your down payment can affect your loan over the long term.

THE PURCHASE AGREEMENT, ATTORNEYS, WARRANTIES, & INSPECTIONS

THE PURCHASE AGREEMENT

When you have found the home of your dreams and made an offer that has been accepted, the next necessary document will be the purchase agreement. This document is a contract between the buyer and the seller outlining how the transaction will proceed. It is important that you understand your rights, remedies, and the consequences of signing this agreement.

The two most important terms in the agreement are the price and the identification of the property. Without these two items, there is no agreement, because it would be too indefinite to enforce. The agreement will contain the common address of the property you are buying, followed by the legal description. While the common address is usually sufficient, it is a good idea to further identify the property by the legal description, which is the identity of the land the house is located on.

From the buyer's perspective, there are several important terms that need to be included in a good purchase agreement:

- **Assurance of good title.** This means that the person purporting to be the owner of the real estate and selling it to you is the real owner. In addition, good title means that there are no title defects; there are no liens on the property other than the seller's mortgage, which will be taken care of at closing. Examples of other liens that affect the seller's title are tax liens, mechanic's liens, judgment liens, and prior unreleased mortgages of record. There can also be problems with the property from easements, zoning ordinances, prior title chain problems, and so on. Title insurance paid for by the seller protects you in case the defect is not found during the title search. If the seller cannot convey good title and the problem is large enough, the buyer can cancel the contract, get his or her money back, and move on to another piece of real estate.

- **Subject to financing.** If you cannot get the financing that you are hoping for, you can get out off going through with the purchase; this does not mean, however, that just because one bank rejects you, you can call off the deal. Most agreements will call for a good faith effort, meaning it is understood that a few banks must reject you before you can cancel the deal. However, this can serve as an out if things are not going as you planned or if you get cold feet.

- **Issuance of a warranty deed.** This is a deed wherein the seller agrees to indemnify you if, down the road, there is a claim that he did not have proper title or someone else had an interest in the property that was not disclosed in the property title search. While this is comforting to have, it does not mean much to the seller, because the title insurance that is purchased will almost always remedy the situation.

The contract will also include a myriad of other terms and conditions to the transfer of the title to the property. It will define:

- **When and where the closing will take place.** This is the time and place that the symbolic transfer of title will occur.

- **Who bears the risk of loss if the property is destroyed before closing.** This almost always falls upon the seller, because they should have homeowner's insurance on the property until they transfer ownership.

- **What fixtures are included in the transfer of the real estate.** Fixtures are the parts of the property that could theoretically be removed, but should never be removed. This would be the carpet, doors, installed bookshelves, and so on. If it is nailed to the property or fixed to the real estate, it stays.

- **What personal property will be conveyed.** This almost always refers to appliances such as the refrigerator, oven, dishwasher, swimming pool, and the like. If you want an item to stay with the house, you need to define this in the purchase agreement. Otherwise, the seller has the right to take it with them.

- **When transfer of possession takes place.** Often the transfer will occur right after the closing and the seller has already moved out. Sometimes you will find a seller that is in the process of buying another house and wishes to remain in the house for a short time after transfer of title. This should be avoided if possible because it does not always work out. Therefore, it is a good idea to put a certain date of possession in the contract with a clause requiring the seller to pay a daily rate until they move out, which increases if they are not out on time.

SHOULD YOU HIRE AN ATTORNEY?

If you do not understand what all these terms mean, you might be wondering whether you should get an attorney to help protect you. The short answer is "yes," but the long answer is "maybe." Yes, you want an attorney if possible; however, real estate brokers and lenders have been lobbying to get attorneys out of the real estate transaction process for several decades.

The Real Estate Bar will tell you that brokers and lenders do not want attorneys coming in and destroying their well-crafted deals, which creates problems for them because it delays their payday by weeks or months, depending on the problems that need to be remedied. Your broker will likely say that attorneys are not necessary because they only complicate matters and cost everyone involved more money. Both sides of the issue have merit, but in almost all states, it is a good idea to at least talk to an attorney about possible representation in a real estate transaction.

Nowhere in this country does the law require an attorney to be involved in the transaction; therefore, the choice is entirely up to you. An attorney can help ensure a hassle-free transaction. If you have been through a few real estate transactions in the past and feel comfortable enough with the process on your own, you might not need an attorney. However, if this is a new experience for you or you are not familiar with how the transaction process works, hire an attorney. This step can save you money in the long term and it will often speed up the process.

Think about the following before you decide that you want to save a few hundred bucks on your six-figure transaction and the biggest asset purchase you will likely ever make:

- Real estate attorneys handle many real estate transactions annually and are familiar with how the process works and the common things that can go wrong.

- They will know most of the people and entities involved and will be able to negotiate the finer details of the transaction. They are also a help in explaining what everything means throughout the process and will make sure you are not getting a bad deal.

- Attorneys will work on a fixed-fee basis, so the cost is often not high compared to the overall transaction; they can also save you thousands of dollars by dealing with an issue before it becomes a problem.

- Attorneys will organize the transaction from the beginning and ensure that the closing goes off without a hitch. They can also negotiate better closing costs in the typical residential real estate transaction.

- Most important, an attorney will be working exclusively for you and will not be getting paid based on whether or not the deal closes, making him a buffer between you and the individuals that will want to push the deal through no matter what. Knowing that your interests will be protected at all times can provide peace of mind.

Given how much can go wrong in a real estate transaction and that most people do not thoroughly understand how the process works, it is a good idea to get an attorney. When you look at the cost-and-benefit analysis and realize that this transaction is one of the biggest any consumer will ever make, it seems silly not to have the help of an experienced professional. However, you will get several opinions from others involved in the transaction that will likely conflict with this advice. It pays to be aware of who is offering their opinions and where their interests truly lie.

Never, under any circumstances, sign a document before you run it by an attorney. If you sign something that does not give you the opportunity to have it reviewed by your attorney, you are stuck with what you signed. So, if you must sign something, make sure it is very conspicuously written on the document that this agreement is subject to attorney review. This will protect you in most circumstances and will allow the attorney to scrutinize it before you are bound by it. This is important for your protection, because sometimes even the best attorney in the world cannot undo a bad contract.

HOW DO YOU FIND A GOOD ATTORNEY?

If you have decided to involve an attorney, there are several places to look for a good one. Most people will go instantly to the yellow pages and call the first person listed under the heading "Attorneys — Real Estate." This technique is fine and will often serve you just as well as any other method. However, there are other ways to find an attorney that might shorten your search.

Call the local bar association, if you have one, or call your state's bar association. Either of these organizations can direct you to an attorney who specializes in real estate. Often you can get the names of a few attorneys and call to find out how much they charge before you make an appointment. Another good method for finding an attorney is talking to friends and family members who might have used one with their own real estate transactions. The appealing aspect to this method is that the people close to you will likely give you an honest assessment of how useful the attorney was.

Once you have identified an attorney, you might want to know what the typical fees are. Unfortunately, depending on where you are located and just how involved your transaction might be, the fees can run a rather large gamut. Most attorneys like to charge by the hour because it does not matter how long or how involved the transaction ends up being; they will still be paid. Hourly rates can vary greatly from one attorney to the other. Some are as low as $100, while others charge as much as $500. Fees often depend on the size of the firm and where it is located. Most solo practitioners and smaller firms in your city will be more reasonable than the big firms.

It is highly advisable that you find an attorney who will charge a flat fee. When you call, ask them whether they will accept a flat fee instead of an hourly rate. It has become customary in some parts of the country to charge a flat fee for all real estate matters. The flat fee might be higher depending on the cost of the real estate or whether or not it is new construction, because expensive homes and new construction involve more of an attorney's time. Flat fees will run anywhere from $300 to $2,000 and can easily be higher. The good thing about flat fees is that they're definite — no matter how much time it takes for the attorney to get the deal closed, the quoted amount is all you pay. Almost always, a flat-fee attorney is the best bang for your buck.

If you have found an attorney, you will want to know whether he is worth it. Set up an initial conference to discuss the transaction and to feel him out. When you meet with him, there are some things to find out before you hire him. First of all, how long has he been handling real estate transactions? How many does he handle in a typical year? You need to get a feel for his experience and how he comes across. If you are satisfied after meeting with him, obtain a copy of his fee agreement contract and tell him you will be in touch. Just because you came to his office and met with him does not obligate you to sign on the dotted line right then and there. Think about it for a few days, ask people if they have ever dealt with him, and then make an informed decision.

NEW-HOME WARRANTIES

Like anything else you buy in this country, you can get a warranty to cover your home purchase. New-home construction is the most typical situation in which you will be offered a warranty, because new homes will have problems that might not be immediately seen. During the first few years, these problems will come to light.

The foundation will be settling for some time to come, and with that settling comes small cracks and other issues. If you buy your home in the middle of summer, you might not use your heat until several months later, which is when you will realize there is a problem with the furnace or heating system. Perhaps your roof will be fine for the first few years, but then the shingles start falling off.

The point is that problems in new-construction homes are inevitable. That is why nearly all home builders will offer a warranty. Some of these warranties simply state that, if something goes wrong within a few years after completing the house, the builder will come back on-site and fix it. Other warranties are through an independent organization that will pay for necessary repairs once you have shown that the problem is the result of faulty construction.

Getting the issue remedied can be a huge headache. Most of the time, the builder will be busy and will shrug off the problems as wear and tear, especially if it has been a few years since the house was completed. This leaves you holding the bag and having to sue the builder to get them to fix the house or pay up. Unfortunately, this is often how the situation plays out, and attorneys are reluctant to get involved in small construction disputes — though if you have major issues, it might be worth your time to sue the builder. In extraordinary cases, suing might be the only option. But builders know that if it is a small problem, the purchaser often will fix it himself and move on.

If you have a warranty through an independent third party, you might face the same kind of problems at first; however, if you persist, most of the time you will get at least a portion of the problem paid for. The key is to make sure you document the problem clearly and concisely with photos and estimates from contractors on what it will take to fix the issue. You might even enlist an attorney's help in writing a letter to the warranty provider.

There might be problems that can be remedied by the individual manufacturers. Nearly all HVAC systems and other major mechanical systems installed in your home will carry their own manufacturer's warranty. If your problem is with the roof or with any of the appliances, they also will likely have a warranty from the manufacturer.

When buying a new-construction home, problems will occur. Make sure your builder is reputable in the community. Ask around; if the builder has been around for a while, you will be able to glean dozens of opinions. Check the local Better Business Bureau for complaints and find out what kind of service it provides.

If the builder refuses to issue any kind of warranty, you can always fall back on the laws of your state for new construction. In nearly all states, there is some form of warranty of habitability, either by statute or by construction of the courts. This is a legal development that protects consumers from shoddy workmanship and sleazy builders. It is a form of consumer protection that can likely be found under your state's version of a consumer protection act.

EXISTING-HOME WARRANTIES

Existing-home warranties are not new, but they have recently become much more popular. These warranties are not like new-construction warranties, which basically cover everything from the top down in the home — they are more of a service contract. An existing-home warranty covers the cost minus the deductible for repairing routine problems within the home. This warranty is also limited in scope. It will cover major items such as the HVAC, appliances, electrical system, and plumbing, but you are on your own for everything else.

It is often the seller that pays for and provides the existing-home warranty for the buyer because the seller wants to just sell the house and move on. Recently, there has been litigation over failure to disclose on the part of the seller; courts, and even the legislature in some states, are putting more of the responsibility for disclosing defects in real estate on the seller of the home. There have been several landmark cases over the last decade in several jurisdictions where this failure to disclose has put the liability for remedying the problem solely on the seller. So to be able to walk away from their home without having to worry about lawsuits in the future, it is worth the cost to buy a warranty for the buyer.

With existing-home warranties, anything that goes wrong, other than specific categories of coverage such as those outlined above, is your responsibility. You will want to go over what is and is not covered in a warranty before you purchase and perhaps even have your attorney review it for exclusions that you haven't considered. Also, if something is not working right or is broken when the title is transferred to you, it will likely not be covered. This would be a problem to address with the seller before closing, because it is their responsibility; the existing-home warranty will not cover a problem that was known at the time of the sale.

Whether an existing-home warranty is something you want to consider is a judgment call. If you are the seller, it is probably worth the cost to keep an issue from causing a headache, and maybe a lawsuit, in the future. If you are the buyer, it does not hurt to ask your representative to provide the warranty. If they say no, you might consider purchasing one yourself — if something goes wrong in the first year, you will be footing the entire bill. More often than not, however, you will not need to use it, and it will be a waste of money.

HOME INSPECTIONS

When you get serious about a house, your broker likely will give you something called a seller's disclosure, a form that will disclose whether the homeowner has had problems with particular items or if he does not know if there are any problems. A seller's disclosure is sometimes required by the broker or by state law. This document can be helpful, but for the most part, it is useless. All it does is let you know that there might have been problems in the past that the homeowner has had to deal with. It does not address problems that might have occurred before the current homeowner owned the home. If the seller has not been there for long, the seller's disclosure is not going to reveal much.

Brokers and sellers are usually required to fill out a seller's disclosure to protect them if there are major defects discovered by the buyer after the closing — they are worried about "undisclosed material latent defects" in the property. This is legalese for something wrong with the house that the owner knew about but did not reveal to the buyer. It is bad if the seller gets caught, because it will likely lead to litigation involving both the broker and the seller. Quite possibly both of these parties will be held liable for misrepresentation. However, that is about the extent of the protection provided by the disclosures.

The only way you can truly protect yourself is to get a home inspection done by a reputable home inspector. There are few exceptions to getting a home inspection done. However, if you are familiar with the property already because you were leasing it or buying it on contract, you likely do not need to bother with the inspection. This is the exception to the rule, however; most other real estate transactions should include a home inspection.

Do yourself a favor and save a lot of money by being vigilant and looking for trouble before you make any substantial offers on a home. A home inspector is often fairly expensive, so you are not going to want to get too many homes inspected. Therefore, carry a checklist with you to each property and rate them with your own amateur inspection, which will help you eliminate problem real estate before you get to the point when a home inspector is called in.

The professional inspection is normally done after you have signed a sales contract for the property. It is also typical to have five days from the signing of the contract to having the inspection completed. If you choose not to buy the house after the inspection, you will be able to get out of the contract if you are within that five-day window.

It is best to be at the inspection with your realtor. This allows both of you to see for yourselves the extent of the damage the inspector finds. The inspector should search for:

- Damage that might require expensive repairs

- Fire, safety, and health hazards

There are seven main areas that the inspector needs to cover: roof, structure, heating, air conditioning, plumbing, electrical, and interior. If there are appliances included in the deal, these should be inspected as well. Always have both the exterior and the interior of the house inspected.

You should also look for the following issues:

- **Houses that stink.** If the house smells bad or certain parts of the house have definite odor issues, it might be in your best interest to pass on the house. A smelly house can be an indication of a myriad of problems; however, the likely culprit is mold. Mold is bad news — it is well known that mold can cause numerous, serious health problems. In addition, cleaning up mold, depending on where it is (e.g., inside the ductwork, behind the drywall in the basement,), can be costly.

- **Basements that are damp, smelly, and/or contain noticeable cracks.** If the basement is damp and smelly, there is a seepage problem. This can mean that the foundation is faulty or that the drainage system has problems. If there are cracks in the basement, it could also indicate that there has been higher-than-normal settling around the foundation, which could mean that it is built on an improperly graded site, among other issues.

- **Wet spots on the ceiling or walls.** These mean that there has been a leak from the roof or from a broken pipe. Unfortunately, many people will paint over these spots, so they might not be readily visible, but if you are really looking, you can still see them.

- **Poor insulation.** Go into the attic and check out the insulation. Observe whether there are any wet areas or dampness. If you notice dampness, you can bet there is a moisture problem, and there might even be dry-rot issues. If everything appears to be dry, check the R factor on the insulation — the higher the number, the better the insulation. If the insulation is not adequate, it could be expensive to heat and cool the house.

- **Improper electrical wiring.** There are a lot of do-it-yourselfers out there, but few know enough to do a good job on electrical wiring. Check the breaker box and see if you notice wires that seem out of place in the basement. If the breaker box is a mess or things do not look right, you might be dealing with a potential problem. This is also a safety concern.

Remember that this inspection is just your own informal screening device; it should never be used in the place of an actual home inspection by a certified professional home inspector. While the house might pass your amateur inspection, there are a number of other issues that will only be noticed by someone familiar with construction and engineering.

HOW DO YOU FIND A HOME INSPECTOR?

The purchase agreement will contain a clause that allows you a certain amount of time to get a home inspection done. This is usually around a week after the signing of the agreement, but it is among the many terms that can be easily negotiated, and most sellers do not mind because they know that this is part of the process. In some instances, you will want to hire a home inspector who will provide a full spectrum of services, such as checking the general condition of the home, as well as for pests, toxic substances, and environmental issues. Most buyers, however, will want to get someone who will just evaluate the general condition of the home. The choice is yours, and we will discuss this shortly.

As with searching for an attorney, the first place just about everyone will look is in their local yellow pages. Doing so will often result in finding a reputable and experienced home inspector. However, you might want to call around for prices and credentials. Ask relatives and friends if they had an inspector they would recommend. Another place you might check is the American Society of Home Inspectors (ASHI), a national organization that has a rigorous process for allowing home inspectors to be members. If the inspector you want to hire is a member of ASHI, he likely is an experienced professional that will do a good job.

When you call an inspector, consider the following to help narrow your choices:

- **Find out what fees they charge.** Fees can vary greatly. Call around to find out what you can expect in your area. Also ask what they include in the inspection. Some inspectors will only do the bare minimum, while others will provide a thorough and detailed inspection for general issues, as well as for pest problems or toxic problems.

- **Find out what type of report they will do.** Some inspectors might just go through the house and use a checklist to identify items that are fair, poor, or in good shape. This is usually not very helpful; as with the disclosures, the information is not that detailed. Ask that the inspector provide a comprehensive report on what he finds, with estimates on replacement costs or how long you might be able to put off getting it repaired or replaced.

- **Find out if the inspector is bonded, insured, and licensed.** Often you will find a number of inspectors who do this type of work part-time. They are contractors or other construction professionals trying to make extra money on the side. While they might be knowledgeable about construction and be able to do a thorough report, they might not be insured, bonded, or licensed, which can become a real problem when you find out later that the inspector missed something expensive or major and you are looking for recourse. The inspector that performs the job on a part-time basis will not have anything beyond his personal assets to back up any liability that might result from his negligence in performing the inspection. You will be left with the responsibility, and the cost, for his mistake.

While it should not be a problem, you need to make sure that the inspector you choose can get to the property before the end of the inspection period. If you wait too long, the buyer has the right to deny the inspector access. It is not hard to get this schedule changed, especially if you have a good attorney, but it is bad form to wait until after the inspection period has passed.

It is also a good idea to be present while the inspector is doing the inspection. Doing so not only helps you ensure that the inspector is doing his job and checking out everything that you want examined, it also helps you learn about the house you are about to buy. By tagging along with the inspector, you can ask him questions directly about problems that he finds and notes; his answers will almost always be more detailed than the answers found in his report. You also can find out just how serious that particular problem is to the inspector and get useful information for how best to remedy the situation.

Here are a few good questions to keep in mind as you walk around with the inspector:

1) How old is my roof, and how long can I expect it to last?

2) Are there any foundation cracks? How many? How severe a problem are they?

3) Is the electrical up to standards?

5) Is the water pressure good on all levels?

6) Can you test for gas leaks?

7) Any signs of termites?

8) How old is my heating and A/C unit?

9) Could you give me an estimated cost of repairs and replacements for items that are found to be defective? This will help to speed up the negotiations on the purchase.

It is important to make sure that they walk the roof, crawl in the crawlspace, climb into the attic, remove the electrical-panel cover, and run the appliances. If they do not, ask them to do so.

Many inspectors include a clause in their contract that basically absolves them of all liability for errors and omissions. If possible, find an inspector that will waive this clause or who does not include it in his contract. If the inspector keeps this clause in the contract, when they are done and you close on the house, you will have no recourse against them.

Use good judgment when you receive the inspection report on your house. Every inspector is going to find something; it might not be earthshaking or a big surprise, but they will find something that will help justify their bill. In a newer house, there likely will be very little that is wrong, while in an older house, there will likely be numerous problems. If you are someone who does not want to put a lot of money into a house, you will want to steer clear of any house that is more than 15 years old — this is the age at which replacement issues begin to come into play. If you are prepared to make expenditures on replacements and repairs in the house, a list of things wrong with the property will not be an unpleasant surprise.

Toxic substances are another concern. In the modern housing market, there are many problems to consider other than construction defects and problems with major appliances and systems. There are issues with radon in many areas of the country; if you have a basement, you should have this checked. An expert can do so, or you can get a test on your own from any local hardware store. Radon is a serious issue, and you should take it seriously — it can cause cancer if the levels are high enough.

Asbestos is another issue in older houses that you should consider checking out. If the house is newer, (i.e., built after the mid-'70s), you might not need to get this checked. If the house is older, you need to get it checked out because, while asbestos undisturbed will not cause any problems, the stigma attached to it from years of massive litigation has turned it into a four-letter word. It will likely cause you to have trouble reselling if you do not take care of it. It can be quite expensive to safely remove asbestos, so if you discover that asbestos is present in the home you are about to buy, it will be worth your while to ask for a credit for the cost of removal. If the seller balks at this proposition, reconsider the purchase.

You also will hear a lot about lead paint, which is similar to the asbestos issue. It is not a problem unless it is disturbed in some way and ingested. If you are buying an older home, it is worth the cost to get it checked out. If lead paint is present, suggest that the cost of removing it be applied as a credit to the purchase price. Once again, if the seller balks, move on to another house.

Suppose your inspector finds something wrong. You have a few choices, depending on what it is he has found. If the problem is fixable, which it will be with 95 percent of the items, you can request that the seller fix the problem before you close the deal. Another option is to reduce the purchase price by the cost of what it would take to fix the problem. If the seller will do neither, you can remove your bid on the house.

If the problem is unfixable (e.g., the water is contaminated, the foundation is severely cracked and unfixable, the house is built over an abandoned mine or fault line), there is not much you can do to change the condition of the property. The question you must then ask yourself is: "Can the seller reduce the price enough for me to feel comfortable buying the property anyway?" If this is not possible in your mind, move on to another property. This problem would be something you had to live with — there would be nothing you could do about it if you chose to buy it anyway. Plus, when you go to resell the property, you are going to face the same problem the seller is facing right now, and that is an uncomfortable position to be in as the seller.

Suppose you close on a home and find out there is a major issue with it that was not disclosed before the purchase. You are going to be facing a rather lengthy and expensive court case. You will also have to prove that the seller and/or broker knew or should have known that the problem existed and disclosed it, which is often hard to prove. Consult an attorney to see whether you have a case that has merit, then prepare for a long, drawn-out legal battle. It is best to protect yourself on the front end by hiring the best home inspection team you can find. You also should do several thorough walkthroughs of the property at different times. If you sit back and rely on the seller's disclosure, you are setting yourself up for a bad situation.

WHAT A HOME BUYER SHOULD NOT EXPECT FROM THE INSPECTOR

An inspector is there to find and examine the scope of the problems; he is not there to fix any of them. He will identify the problem so that you can have it corrected, either through the purchase negotiations or after you have purchased the property.

The inspector is not there to tell you whether you should buy the house — that decision is up to you. Some defects are minor and easily remedied, like light switches not up to code or windows and doors that need resealing. However, major issues, like structural issues and termite problems, can be expensive to resolve, in which case you might want to rethink the purchase.

There is also no guarantee that what worked while the inspection was taking place will still be working when you move in. A home inspection can only identify any problems that exist at the time of the inspection.

ESCROW, PMI POINTS, & PROPERTY TAX

ESCROW

A common part of any mortgage transaction is the requirement of an escrow account for real estate taxes and homeowner's insurance. An escrow account is an account set up and maintained by the financial institution. Every month, part of your mortgage payment is deposited into this account, which works much like a checking account that you cannot access, except for two payments a year for taxes and insurance.

It is required by all lenders that these accounts be set up and funded by your monthly payment. Your lender can do this because all states have enacted a law allowing this practice. They also put in safeguards to make sure that the lender does not abuse this procedure.

Escrow came about mainly to protect the lender from the problems associated with a real estate tax lien on secured property. A tax lien has priority over any other liens on the property, no matter when they are recorded. Therefore, if a lender takes a first mortgage on your property and you do not pay the taxes on that property, if the lender is forced to foreclose, the proceeds of the sale will go first to pay the tax lien, which will cause the lender to recoup less money on the foreclosure sale and not get as much to pay toward the outstanding loan. This is reason enough for a lender to require that the escrow account be established to make sure that the taxes are paid.

This benefits the borrower as well because it makes it possible to budget the large expense of real estate taxes, reducing the chance that a homeowner will be surprised by a large tax bill at the end of the year. It also simplifies the payment process so that the owner does not have to deal with paying the taxes — the lender takes care of this.

While your money sits in the escrow account all year, the lender makes interest on that money. This practice is always a hot topic between borrowers and lenders. Lenders say that this helps offset the administrative costs of maintaining so many different accounts; borrowers say that the lenders are taking money from them. Both are right, but there is not any current legislation that will push it one way or the other.

A lender is limited by law to holding only two months more than a full year's worth of escrowed taxes. This law went into effect in the early 90s because some lenders were taking advantage of escrow accounts and requiring large upfront deposits, which were sometimes several years' worth of real estate taxes. This was too much for the legislature to sanction, so they put a stop to the practice. If a lender tells you this is not the case, you should probably find another lender.

If you do not want an escrow account and would like to pay the taxes on your own, it is possible to do this, but you will have to have almost 30 percent equity built up in your house before you can make this request. If you do not have the 30 percent equity, you can get an escrow-free loan by pledging something as security for the taxes, such as a savings account, certificate of deposit, or stock that has enough value to cover the expense. It is also possible to find a lender that does not require escrow without either of the first two options; however, the lender will make it up somewhere else in the loan, often in the form of a 2 percent fee for the amount of the loan.

Escrow is not a bad process. In some instances, it works out well and reduces the headache of scraping together enough money to pay your taxes at the end of the year.

Homeowner's insurance escrow is similar to real estate tax escrow. This account is set up for the sole purpose of making sure that the homeowner's policy is fully paid and that the acceptable amount of coverage is in place. This particular aspect of the mortgage goes to protect both the lender and the borrower equally. The lender wants to make sure that the security for its loan is protected, and that if anything happens, it will be able to recoup the loss. The buyer is interested because they want to protect their investment and the equity that they build up in the house. For more on the particulars of coverage, please review the section on insurance.

When you reach the equity threshold — in this instance, 30 percent or more — you can request that the escrow be terminated. Many people do not bother to do this when they reach that point, and there is no good reason to end it if you do not want to. But if you are interested in saving money on your mortgage, this is an area that you will want to watch. You do not make interest on your escrow account — the bank does. If you want to make sure that you are keeping and making as much money as possible from your investment, and if you are fiscally responsible, you can save the money for real estate taxes and homeowner's insurance in your own high-interest account. By doing this you will make the interest on the money, not the bank. This might not be a huge amount of money monthly, but over the years, it will add up.

PRIVATE MORTGAGE INSURANCE

Private mortgage insurance (PMI) is often associated with mortgages that are riskier than others. The lender will require a 20 percent down payment to keep you from having to pay PMI, and it might be required by law in your state. Without this insured protection, the lender will be unable to resell the loan on the secondary market, making it an unattractive proposition.

PMI is insurance taken out on a loan to protect the lender from losing money in the transaction. It is common knowledge in the mortgage industry, and statistics have shown, that people who cannot afford to put up at least 20 percent are more likely to default. Therefore, if you do not have the money for a 20 percent down payment, you are a risk that lenders might not be willing to take. Whether this is fair or not, the industry and legislators have decided that both buyers and lenders need protection from the costs of a potential foreclosure.

PMI is designed to step in and cover the spread between what you get out of the house from foreclosure and what is still owed on the loan. Technically, this protects both sides, but it is more geared toward protecting the lender from losses accrued from the legal expenses of foreclosure. However, without PMI a lot of potential buyers would be shut out of owning a home. While PMI does cost a lot, it at least gives those who cannot save up the 20 percent down payment the opportunity to buy a house and begin building some equity, albeit slowly. In addition, the interest on a mortgage is tax deductible — a benefit not available to a renter.

You might be able to find a lender that is willing to loan you the money for a house that does not include PMI. If you are considering such an option, do your homework, because these lenders usually make up the risk by charging more interest over the life of the loan. To make sure that you will not get 20 percent equity and then refinance, the lender often will stick in a prepayment penalty. Use caution and sound judgment when you explore this possibility.

PMI is also a hot issue that has been addressed through litigation because it was often abused by unscrupulous lenders. Today a lender must explain to you at closing how to cancel your PMI when you have reached the 20 percent equity threshold. The lender must also inform you annually that, if you reach the 20 percent equity threshold, you can cancel the PMI.

You can be proactive about this and save money. The best way to do this is to be vigilant about how much you have paid in principal on your loan and how much your home is going up in value. If you are in an area where real estate prices are skyrocketing, it would be worth your time to explore what the value of your home is. If the value has gone up significantly and you have been making the principal payment, you might be surprised at how close you are to reaching 20 percent equity.

If you think that you have reached this benchmark, getting your house appraised will be a good investment. If you have reached the 20 percent threshold, you can take it to your lender and they must cancel your PMI. If you are not this proactive, you can wait until you are at 22 percent equity, at which point your lender must cancel your PMI.

You should be proactive in canceling your PMI as soon as possible, however, because this is money you are paying on a monthly basis that is being wasted. If you can get the PMI canceled, that is money you can start putting toward your principal, which will cost you less and help you pay off your house more quickly.

There is also a way that you can get a loan without PMI that does not involve paying more interest or getting stuck with an expensive prepayment penalty loan. You can get "creative financing." If you have some money for a down payment, but not nearly enough for 20 percent, lenders will work with you. Let us explore the various forms of creative financing.

There is an 80/10/10 or an 80/15/5 loan. These products allow you to put up 10 percent, or even 5 percent, and avoid the PMI because you will essentially be getting two loans. The first loan will be for 80 percent of the purchase price, and the second will be for 10 or 15 percent, depending on your down payment. The second loan is a home equity loan that basically will make up the difference you are missing on the down payment.

The problem with these structures is that the home equity loan is usually an in-house loan at the financial institution that you have chosen. Home equity loans almost always charge a higher interest rate than regular mortgage loans. If you elect to use this as your financing method, make sure that you will be able to pay off the home equity portion of the loan quickly. Otherwise, you might end up worse off than if you just paid the PMI, since the extra interest will eat up any savings quickly.

PMI is not as bad as some would have you believe, and it can be a useful tool for lenders and buyers alike. The trick is to make sure that you are doing what is best for you, given your financial situation. If you just cannot stomach paying PMI, you have options and you should explore all of them carefully before you jump into a bad situation. If you want to save money, you need to avoid PMI because it does nothing to help you build equity.

PROPERTY TAXES

Real estate taxes will be assessed on your home, and there is little you can do to change this. At least check to make sure your property has been assessed correctly according to whatever property tax formula your state might follow. Doing so is easy if you go to your local assessor's office and ask some questions. If you are satisfied that your house has been assessed correctly for property tax purposes, you have done all you can to lower your bill. If, however, you discover a discrepancy or you think the assessor is wrong, it might be worth your time to discuss the issue with a local tax attorney. You might have some recourse and be able to get the tax liability on your home reduced to reflect the proper value under the law.

If you are an older individual or a person who is disabled, you might have other options to reduce your property tax liability. You should check with your assessor's office to find out about any homestead exemption you might be entitled to claim. Depending on the assessed value of your home, this might reduce your tax liability to zero. It is worth checking out, and most of the time, if you do not bring it to the attention of the tax officials, it will not get properly credited.

POINTS — WHAT ARE THEY?

One point is equivalent to 1 percent of the loan amount. For example, for a $300,000 mortgage, one point would be $3,000. You can receive a lower mortgage rate if you pay a point up front. There is an added benefit in that mortgage points are considered a form of prepaid interest by the IRS. This means that mortgage points can be deducted from taxable income.

SHOULD YOU PAY POINTS?

By paying points, you are actually paying interest in an upfront lump sum in exchange for a lower rate on a fixed-rate mortgage. Therefore, if you want a lower interest rate, you can pay more points up front.

But which is better — more points and a lower interest rate, or no points and a higher rate?

To make this decision, consider the following:

1. Can you afford the upfront payment of the points?

2. How long are you planning on keeping the house? The longer

you are planning to stay there, the more you will save with the points-upfront option, and you will reap the benefits from the lower interest rate over a long time.

WHY NOT PAY POINTS MORE OFTEN?

Due to the insecurity of the future, not everyone relies on staying in their home for the long term. People lose jobs, change partners, have families, or refinance. With any and all of these changes happening in people's lives all the time, not everyone wants to pay money up front. Statistics show that if you make a down payment of less than 20 percent, there is reason to believe you will refinance within the first three years of your mortgage.

Points have gained a bad reputation for several reasons. One is because homeowners can end up paying for points without knowing it. The term "point" is often used interchangeably with the terms "loan origination fee," "loan discount," and "discount points." Therefore, it is important to look over your closing-cost breakdown (good faith estimate). Check to see if there are any points included. If there is a $2,000 loan origination fee, along with several other costs, you might not think anything of it, especially if it is your first time buying a house and you know there will be many closing costs, but do not necessarily know which ones. However, that $2,000 loan origination fee is the same as a "point." And it might not be getting you a lower mortgage rate and might be an unnecessary closing cost.

The easiest way to find out is to ask your loan officer if you are paying any points. Make sure you check over your closing costs and have your real estate attorney do the same at closing.

THE DOWN PAYMENT

A down payment is the amount of money presented at the beginning of a loan to demonstrate commitment and means toward the loan. It is usually given as cash, but it can be attached to a line of credit. In some cases, property can be the down payment. The financing costs of a loan have no effect on the down payment.

Let us take a closer look. The down payment is the difference between the amount of the loan and the cost of the property. If the value of the house is $250,000, and you have a loan of $200,000, then your down payment would be $50,000. In this case, this down payment works out to 20 percent, so you will not need to purchase private mortgage insurance. If you had only $45,000 and needed to up the loan to $205,000, then your down payment would drop below the 20 percent and you would need to purchase private mortgage insurance.

Land can be used as a down payment if you own the land and want to have a house built on it. In this case, if the builder is going to build you a $200,000 house and the appraisal comes in at $300,000, then the land is assumed to be worth $100,000. This holds true if you have held the land for several years. If, however, it is a new purchase, the lender will not assess a value greater than what you paid for it.

It is common for family members to help each other out with down payments, especially parents helping their children buy their first homes. Lenders will accept a parent's gift of equity as the equivalent of a cash down payment. By following IRS rules, gift taxes can be avoided.

SIZE OF THE DOWN PAYMENT

For many people, there is little or no choice about the down payment they can make. For those who are purchasing with no down payment, there is no decision to make. If you have less than 20 percent to put down, you are required to buy private mortgage insurance. To avoid this, many borrowers are taking second mortgages to avoid the extra insurance. Therefore, it makes sense to put down the 20 percent down payment if you can.

If you have more than 20 percent for a down payment, you might wonder whether you should put everything down that you can. This question brings up many other topics regarding investing your money, rate of return, and mortgage payments as tax deductions to lower income versus investment income, which raise your taxes.

Speak with a financial advisor. With today's volatile market, the answers can change daily. Find someone who can help you make the right decision to maximize your returns while minimizing your investment risks.

SECTION

3

THE MORTGAGE

After you have determined what your situation requires and you have familiarized yourself with some of the other variables of the mortgage equation, you are ready to begin collecting all the remaining information that will aid in your plan and teach you how to save thousands of dollars on your mortgage.

In **Chapter 7,** we introduce you to mortgages and the history of how the system came about. In **Chapter 8,** we provide an overview of the entire process. In **Chapter 9,** we provide you with information about where you should begin your search for mortgage information: banks, mortgage companies, the Internet, even the U.S. government.

Chapter 10 is a detailed examination of the mortgage industry. It contains an in-depth look at mortgage structuring, markets, and how lenders influence available loan options. This chapter is one of the most important sections of the book. To capitalize on your mortgage options, you must have an understanding of the inner workings of a somewhat secretive and almost always complicated purchasing process.

In **Chapter 11,** we provide you with an overview of the many programs available and tell you where to look for more detailed information about each one.

In **Chapter 12,** we examine the many mortgage lenders and how your lender choice affects your mortgage options.

In **Chapter 13,** we provide you with the information you will need to collect the pieces that complete your financial picture, as viewed by a mortgage lender.

WHAT IS A MORTGAGE?

A mortgage is actually two documents that work together to make it possible to buy something as expensive as a house when you do not have the money to do so up front. The first document is the promissory note, which is the negotiable instrument that can be transferred. The mortgage is a separate document that represents the security interest for the note — the collateral.

To get the promissory note, you must have property that is worth at least as much as the amount borrowed; in the case of a house, that would be the real estate. The mortgage is a document that signifies that the note is secured by collateral of equal value. No lender will give you the amount of money necessary to buy a house without making sure that it is secured by some other property of value. For instance, in the case of a car loan, the lender is secured by the automobile you purchase. If you do not pay the loan back, they have the right to repossess the car to recoup most of their money back.

MORTGAGE HISTORY

One of the best ways to understand the mortgage industry is by understanding its history. Mortgages are commonplace today, and they originated as far back as the 12th century. Despite the number of years this system has been in place, the basics remain the same.

In early England, a mortgage was a conditional sale in which the law would protect the creditor by giving him an interest in his debtor's property. Although the creditor held the title on this property, the debtor could sell the property to recover his money in the event that the debt was not paid.

As immigrants came to America, they brought this system with them. By the early 1900s, mortgages were already widespread and land ownership continued to increase. However, not everyone was in a position to purchase land outright or obtain a mortgage. Back then, a purchaser was often required to pay 50 percent down on a five-year mortgage. The final amount would have been complete with the monthly installments or would have been required at the end of the five years.

This is the way the system continued through to the Great Depression, when it collapsed. By this point, the lenders had no money to lend and borrowers had no money to pay.

It was during Franklin D. Roosevelt's presidency when things turned around. He introduced laws and institutions to stimulate the economy. With these new laws, the mortgage system was restructured and mortgages were available to all Americans.

The Federal Housing Administration (FHA) was created in 1934. Its purpose was to insure mortgage lenders against losing money from defaulting buyers and to provide a 30-year fixed-rate loan, allowing buyers to have stability and affordable payments.

This system worked, but with problems — there was not always enough money for the lenders to lend, and there were inconsistent loan and interest rates, as these were set according to individual economies. This meant adjustments to the system were necessary.

This brought about the creation of the Federal National Mortgage

Association (FNMA), otherwise known as Fannie Mae. This association purchased FHA-insured loans and sold them again as securities on the money market. This kept mortgage-lending funds flowing and created a "hidden" secondary mortgage market.

A fairer and more efficient mortgage system was also attributed to Fannie Mae as central guidelines were established. These guidelines required the lenders' compliance if they wanted to sell their loans to the secondary market.

Then came the Second World War. The war changed the mortgage scene and the economy as a whole as veterans came home to enter the work force. These veterans led the consumerism push, and one of the items they wanted to buy was a home. To help them out, the Veterans Administration was given the right to guarantee mortgage loans to veterans in 1944, allowing military personnel to buy homes without a down payment. The housing market exploded, as did the need for mortgages.

Change happened again when women entered the work force, creating two-income families. These families (baby boomers) wanted fancier, larger homes to fit their life styles. Larger mortgages were required, and in greater numbers.

Enter Freddie Mac, another name for the Federal Home Loan Mortgage Corporation (FHLMC). Freddie Mac was created to increase the mortgage funds available to banks and other mortgage lenders, thereby creating more available funds for people.

At that time, and through the 1950s and '60s, mortgage terms were normally 20 to 30 years. That worked until the interest rates rose too high (20 percent-plus) for most people. It was then that the mortgages were reduced to a one-, three-, or even rarer five-year term. Banks were also finally allowed to write out mortgages during this time.

Fast forward to the late 1990s, when the five-year mortgage dropped to less than 7 percent. Today banks are responsible for more than 63 percent of the outstanding mortgages.

With this massive amount of money riding on mortgages, more systems have been developing over the years to establish whom to lend money to. Nobody wanted to have defaulting loans. This produced the credit system currently in place today, where a credit bureau monitors your credit, meaning how you handle your financial obligations. Good credit offered a lending institute a better chance of having the buyer make good on his mortgage payments.

To keep the system stable, there needs to be a healthy balance and cash flow. If there are too many defaults on mortgages, the system will become unstable. The industry is constantly changing and improving, allowing mortgage availability to lower-income families, single parents, and individuals.

COMMERCIAL MORTGAGES

These are similar to residential or home mortgages, except they are for commercial property, which is defined as a property used for business purposes, such as stores, industrial buildings, office buildings, golf courses, resorts, hotels, even garages. Commercial loans can also be used on commercial property under construction.

You can find many of the same loan options for commercial property as for residential property. The same principles apply to commercial mortgages as to residential mortgages, but the collateral is business property.

There is one difference between commercial versus residential properties — interest rates are usually lower for commercial properties.

For a commercial loan, you still go through the same process as you would with any other mortgage. You still need to do your research and make an educated decision.

Lenders will want more details about the commercial venture — what kind of business you are in, business plans, and business records, if there are any, that will support the viability of your business.

You might have more difficulty getting a mortgage for a commercial property versus a residential property, but there will still be many options. You might have to pay a slightly higher interest rate to get the mortgage, but you should still be able to get one.

You can always consider a mortgage broker. They will work with you to find a lender. Again, do your research to ensure you are getting a reasonably fair deal and that the broker is working in your best interests.

WALKING THROUGH THE MORTGAGE PROCESS

The mortgage process can seem intimidating, especially for first-time home buyers. However, it can be simplified by breaking it down into its most basic elements. A step-by-step analysis is the best way to understand how to obtain a mortgage.

STEP 1: PAPERWORK

The first step you take in the mortgage process, before even meeting with a loan officer, is to gather all the necessary paperwork. This is important to assist your lender in setting up your mortgage and to allow you to evaluate your own financial situation and how a mortgage for the purchase of a new home will affect it. Having a complete set of all relevant information, organized and up-to-date, will make the mortgage process more efficient, preventing delays and the resulting stress that can result from missing information.

You and, if applicable, your co-mortgagor, should put together a file of the originals and at least one copy of the following documents, so that you and your lender have paper records of all relevant information:

- **Tax returns.** Make sure you have at least your last two tax returns. This information will paint a picture of your financial situation, including your income and tax liabilities — in short, your ability to pay back any mortgage you are granted. You might worry that revealing your personal or household income to potential lenders will diminish the amount of the mortgage you are able to secure, but banks, mortgage companies, and other lenders are in the business of making money, so they will be eager to loan you the most money they feel you will be able to pay back to them with interest. Of course, do your own research as well so that you know what amount of mortgage you should be looking for. However, do not be discouraged if what you are offered is less than what you feel you should be able to borrow. You can always shop around with other lenders or look into alternative creative financing solutions to get the house that is right for you.

- **Pay stubs.** As with tax returns, lenders will analyze your paycheck stubs to determine how much of a mortgage you likely are able to pay back. In your document file, you should include at least your last two to three pay stubs, especially if your income varies from pay period to pay period, since a single stub might over- or underestimate your true average income, thereby skewing the analysis of what size mortgage you are eligible for. Furthermore, the lender will want to determine whether you have been regularly employed and whether your income stream is reliable and steady. If you have more than one job or have income from any other source that you are free to use for repayment of the mortgage plus applicable interest, such as a settlement payout or pension, include evidence of that income as well to better illustrate your full financial picture.

- **Bank statements.** Bank statements are one more tool a lender will use to put together a complete picture of your financial situation. Providing you with a mortgage will seem like a less risky proposition to a lender if you can demonstrate you have some money in the bank. First, savings are a safety cushion; funds reflected on your bank statement are insurance that you have reserves with which to pay the money you owe the lender in the event that your income changes. Furthermore, a healthy savings account reflects well on you as a borrower, indicating that you are responsible and capable of money management. You should have at least your last two bank statements ready. Mortgage lenders understand that not everyone is able to build up a substantial reserve, especially new home buyers. Other things that lenders look for in bank statements are bounced checks or any other anomalies that could be a red flag about your ability to fulfill your repayment commitment.

- **Bankruptcy documents.** If you have bankruptcy in your history, make sure your file includes all bankruptcy documents. Do not try to hide a past bankruptcy for fear you will look bad; lenders understand that people sometimes have no other option but to file for bankruptcy and remain receptive to those who have bounced back from dire financial situations. Plus, because bankruptcy is a matter of public record, any lender will run a check and find out the truth anyway. If you have been discharged from bankruptcy, ensure that you have your discharge records available. A rebound from bankruptcy can demonstrate to a lender that you have made strides in your financial life and that you have become more financially responsible post-bankruptcy.

- **Divorce documents and child support orders.** If you have been recently divorced or if you are paying alimony or child support, be sure to include relevant papers in your file of documents.

Lenders use this type of information to better understand how much money you have coming in and going out on a regular basis. In addition, any agreements that require you to pay some or all of a previous mortgage on which a former spouse is a co-borrower will assist in the analysis of how much mortgage you can afford in the purchase of your new home.

Any other documents that can more completely establish your financial situation should also be included. Remember, the mortgage amount and interest rate you are ultimately offered will depend on information about your income and expenses; the more information you make available, the better equipped the lender will be to provide you with the best mortgage.

If you cannot find some of the necessary documentation, do not be alarmed — many people cannot find their tax returns from two years ago. Fortunately, the above-referenced documents can be obtained fairly easily.

If you need copies of your tax returns, get them from your accountant, if you had one who prepared your taxes, or from your employer during the tax period in question — employers are required by law to provide you with this information, so do not take no for an answer. Alternatively, you can order a copy from the Internal Revenue Service (IRS) by visiting the IRS Web site at **www.irs.gov** and downloading and completing Form 4506. The completed form must be mailed to the included address, along with a processing fee, which is currently $39. The IRS suggests allowing at least 60 days for a response, so if you are unable to obtain your tax documents in another way and must resort to this approach, allow plenty of time before you must provide the information to your lender.

Pay stubs can be obtained from your employer. Employers are legally required to provide you with copies upon request. For bank statements, request that your bank print them out for you and stamp or otherwise authorize them to indicate that they are official documents from the bank.

Banks often charge a fee for the copies.

Other documents, such as bankruptcy or divorce papers, can be obtained at the courthouse in the jurisdiction where the bankruptcy or divorce order was filed. Again, you might be charged a copy fee. Alternatively, if an attorney was involved, you can approach him or her for copies of the applicable documents; note, however, that if the action was filed more than a few years ago, the documents could take some time to locate, or the files could have been destroyed altogether. The time for which attorneys maintain closed files varies, but you should be notified before destruction of the file.

Most lenders will request your financial documents in advance to look them over and prepare an analysis that they will present to you at your first meeting.

STEP 2: FIRST CONTACT

Your first meeting with a mortgage lender might be in person, although in light of the current prevalence of technological advances and Internet transactions, it is just as likely to be online. There might be benefits, depending on your situation, to applying online.

Whether in person or online, your first meeting with a mortgage representative will involve a series of questions about your finances, including your past and current work situations, any issues evident from the paperwork you provided, the status of your credit report, and similar issues.

After reviewing the documentation you provided and getting additional information from your answers to questions, the lender will be able to establish more clearly just how much you can realistically afford. Subsequently, the lender will provide you with information about the type and amount of mortgage you qualify for; often, there will be more than one option, so make sure you conduct your own research about the advantages and disadvantages of each approach.

When you are certain about the particular mortgage that is right for you, you will complete a formal loan application form, which can be completed at home or at work. Take your time; the reading is dry, but well worth your time to make sure you truly understand what you are signing. If you have any questions while filling out the form, contact the lender for clarification.

When you have completed the application form, sign it and return it to the lender, along with all the supporting documents you previously collected. Keep a complete copy of the application and all documents for your own file.

STEP 3: PROCESSING

The processing of your application is the next step in the mortgage process. The person who handles your mortgage application is called a loan processor, and he or she might be your loan officer or an entirely separate third party. The processor is a liaison between you and the lender; he or she, or sometimes a team of processors, will make sure your application is complete and will provide all the necessary information to the lender. For example, the processor might ask you for new information or additional paperwork, coordinate your appraisal and home inspection, and handle other tasks that will help make the mortgage process efficient and beneficial to you and the lender, including facilitating communication between you and the lender.

STEP 4: PREAPPROVAL

Assuming everything is in order and the lender approves providing you with a mortgage, you will be preapproved. This status of preliminary approval gives you leverage to negotiate with the seller of a house in which you are interested. You should give copies of your preapproval documents to your real estate agent so that he or she can share with the seller or his or her real estate agent that you have already met the qualifications to buy a home. Home sellers are more willing to deal with prospective buyers who are already guaranteed to have the money for purchase available.

STEP 5: APPRAISAL

An appraisal is an estimate of what the property you are interested in is worth. The appraisal, performed by a professional, licensed, or certified appraiser, is based on the "highest and best use" of the property — in other words, the use that makes the land the most valuable. The appraiser will examine the house and the land, as well as any relevant paperwork that might reveal aspects of the property that are not obvious.

The value produced by the appraiser will be used by your lender to help determine how much of a mortgage you should receive; the lender, understandably, will not want to loan you money in excess of what you will need for the home purchase, because in the event that you do not repay your loan and face foreclosure, the lender's potential recovery will be limited by the value of the property.

Some mortgage lenders have appraisers on their staff; others regularly employ reputable independent appraisers. Regardless, in most instances, you as the home buyer will end up paying for the appraisal fees, which are usually rolled into your final payment settlement at the real estate closing.

STEP 6: INSPECTIONS

Home inspections are a crucial step in the mortgage process. Many cities require inspections; even where a home inspection is not required, every home buyer should hire a reputable inspector to check the home for structural and environmental integrity and electrical and plumbing issues. A professional evaluation of your future home is not only beneficial for your own peace of mind, but it is also a sound investment in the future of your home and your finances.

An inspector will check the land, the roof, the fixtures, the electrical wiring, the plumbing, and the rest of your future home to make sure everything is in proper working order and appropriately constructed. He or she will inform you of any problems, usually categorizing them as critical or aesthetic, so that you know what you are getting into in terms of property remediation and monetary expense to make your new house a home in which you feel secure and comfortable. An inspector also will evaluate the home for potential health hazards, such as asbestos-based insulation or lead-based paint. Some areas require, or home buyers might choose to have, termite or insect inspections.

Fees vary depending on the type of inspection, the location, the individual inspector, and other factors. Required inspections must take place before the mortgage for a particular home is finalized, and optional inspections elected by the home buyer should also be completed before signing for a loan. Inspection results will help you determine whether the amount of your mortgage truly reflects the value of the home you want to buy and will shed light on any issues that could compromise your financial situation, such as major necessary or prospective repairs.

STEP 7: TITLE SEARCH AND INSURANCE

"Title" refers to ownership of a specific parcel of land. When you own a home, you are said to have title to the house and the land on which it sits. Title belongs to your mortgage lender until you complete the payoff of your mortgage. When buying a house, your lender will require that a title search be conducted on the property you are interested in. This search is conducted by a title company and verifies that the person selling the property has the right to do so. This way, you and the lender are protected against the possibility that there might be someone out there who can subsequently claim ownership of all or part of the property.

Once it is established that title to the land is in order, you will be required to secure title insurance. Title insurance protects you against financial loss and the possible expense of having to defend your title to the property in court. The cost of the insurance is often included in the final settlement you reach with your lender, and title insurance documents are signed with your other purchase documents at the closing.

STEP 8: FINAL APPROVAL

Once you have gone through all the preceding steps, an underwriter who works for your lender will make the ultimate decision regarding whether you qualify for a loan and will finalize the loan amount. At this point, you will receive what is called a loan commitment — documentation that proves you will get your mortgage and in what amount. At this stage, you are clear to close — ready to buy your new home.

STEP 9: CLOSING

In preparation for closing, you must secure homeowner's insurance. Homeowner's insurance must be paid at the outset for the first full year, and your lender will probably require that you have evidence of payment, in the form of a hard-copy document, available at closing.

The actual closing might take place at your title company, at the business of your lender, at the office of an attorney (if one is involved), or at some other location agreed on by you, the seller of the house you are buying, and the title company. In most instances, your real estate agent and/or loan officer will be present.

At the closing, you will sign all relevant documents; this adds up to a lot of paperwork and can be tiring and time consuming. Stay focused. The title officer will explain what each document is and what it means to sign it. If you have any questions during this process, do not hesitate to ask. A home purchase is a major endeavor, a huge financial responsibility, and an event that will have an enormous impact on your life — you deserve to have the best and most complete information explained to you in terms you can understand. Remember, this will be your money spent on your home — you have not only the right but also the obligation to be well informed.

The closing is when the actual transfer of money occurs, as well as the symbolic transfer of the property itself. Any money you are required to bring will have to be in the form of a certified check. Once the papers are signed and the money has changed hands, you will receive the keys to your new house. Congratulations — all your hard work will have paid off and you can embark on your new life in your new home.

WHERE TO LOOK: BANKS, MORTGAGE COMPANIES, THE INTERNET, & THE GOVERNMENT

The real estate market goes up and down in cycles, but there will always be demand for homes. Few people can afford to buy a house outright with cash, so mortgages are a big business. It should come as no surprise, therefore, that there is a multitude of resources available to home buyers seeking loans.

In this chapter, we will discuss the various options you have when seeking money for the purchase of a home. We will cover the advantages and disadvantages of using each of the available resources, including mortgage companies, banks, credit unions, private individuals, the government, and even the Internet. You should explore each of the options as it pertains to your specific situation to determine which route is best for you.

There is one important question to ask before you make your final choice: Is it stable?

How can you tell if your lender is stable? Go to the large rating companies to check. Six credit agencies will give you information about financial strength. You can do this online:

- **www.ambest.com**   A.M. Best

- **www.duffllc.com**   Duff & Phelp

- **www.fitchratings.com**   Fitch, Inc.

- **www.moodys.com**   Moody's Investors Service

- **www.standardandpoors.com** Standard & Poor's

- **www.weissratings.com**   Weiss Ratings

These companies look at factors concerning the financial performance of an organization. If you are dealing with a small lender, it is possible they have not been rated. Therefore, you will have to do the research yourself. Check first with the Better Business Bureau in your area to see if there are any complaints. You can also talk to other clients from the company and hear firsthand what they experiences were.

Do not be attracted to a good interest rate to the point that you overlook the company's stability. If they have problems, you could end up in foreclosure. Be smart up front and plan for your future.

MORTGAGE BROKERS

Do not confuse a mortgage broker with a mortgage company. Mortgage brokers are independent real estate financial professionals who specialize in finding the best mortgage for their customers, either residential or commercial.

Just as a realtor specializes in bringing a homeowner and a home buyer together, a mortgage broker specializes in bringing lenders and borrowers together.

In the United States, the borrower is usually the one who pays the broker's fees; therefore, the fees need to be discussed and understood up front. You want the broker to be working for you and not working to raise his fees by going for the higher option.

Brokers have access to many lenders, with a wide selection of loans for you to choose from. They will contact the lenders on your behalf to get you the best deal if you have signed a contract with them. If you have not signed a contract, they are not obligated in the same way. If you choose to not sign a contract, work with several brokers for mortgage quotes to ensure that you will be shown the best options.

Since brokers make more money the larger the loan, make sure you are not being talked into a mortgage that is too large for you to handle over the long term. Their interest might lie in the larger commission and not with your needs.

Broker's fees average 1.7 percent (in 2004) of the total loan amount. This brings up an important factor: yield spread premium. This is where the interest rate is raised on the mortgage amount, and in exchange the lender will pay some or all of the broker's fees.

The problem with this is that dishonest brokers will ask for the interest rate increase without the customer requesting it and the broker will still get the fee from the lender, which he does not pass on to the buyer, and he still gets the fee from the buyer. In essence, he is paid twice.

To protect yourself, watch for extra fees paid by the lender and listed on the closing statements. Fees that the lender paid to the broker will appear as "paid outside closing" (POC). These are often listed in a different place.

It is also smart to ask if your broker is receiving any fees in exchange for raising your interest rate. If this is the case, then the fee you pay your broker should be reduced by the same amount as any POC fees.

MORTGAGE COMPANIES

Mortgage companies issue more than half of all real estate loans made in the United States. The popularity of mortgage companies as a home loan resource is a result of these companies' specialization; because real estate lending is all they do, the mortgage brokers employed by these companies are, for the most part, extremely knowledgeable and competent.

Mortgage companies, through individual brokers, act as liaisons between the home buyers who borrow money for their purchase and the lenders who issue the mortgage for that purpose. Mortgage brokers work with specific lenders, so your source of money will depend on which mortgage company you choose. However, this is unlikely to be an issue, since large, reputable mortgage companies are associated with a multitude of lenders, allowing them to find a true match for each individual borrower with whom they do business.

Mortgage companies almost always charge fees for their services. These fees are sometimes paid by the borrower, sometimes by the lender, and sometimes split between the parties. Whatever portion of the fee you, as the borrower, are responsible for will be rolled into the total amount you pay at closing.

Some mortgage brokers use an "upfront" system, which means that they negotiate a flat fee directly with the borrower at the beginning of the relationship in exchange for a promise to shop for the lowest interest rate available to the home buyer. If you elect to work with a mortgage broker who operates under an upfront payment system, be sure that you are truly getting the best deal available. Just because the broker is committed to finding the best interest rate for you does not mean that you should give up control entirely; if you find a better deal than what the broker has offered, or if you are suspicious about his or her actions, report him or her to a supervisor at the mortgage company. This is your house, your loan, and your responsibility — retain control and stay informed so you get the best possible deal.

As for the differences between a bank, credit union, or finance company, it comes down to the interest rate you will get, the services that are included, and whether you will qualify with the lender for a mortgage. It is worth checking out big and small lenders in your hunt for a mortgage. It is also worth being preapproved by more than one type of lender, to compare the kinds of services and interest rates you could get. Even a difference of 1 percent could save you hundreds, if not thousands, over the life of a mortgage.

BANKS

Banks tend to be the first place people think of when they think of a mortgage.

Banks are everywhere. Some of the larger banks with a nationwide presence include Bank of America, Chase, Citigroup, and Wells Fargo. These institutions offer a variety of services, and their primary source of business is not mortgage loans, although all the major commercial banks do offer this service.

The main benefit of securing your mortgage through a bank is that banks often offer competitive interest rates. Because their business is broader than just home loans, banks can afford to offer lower rates to customers. Furthermore, you might find that if you do your other, nonmortgage banking with a particular institution, the familiarity that particular bank has with you can work in your favor. Not only will the mortgage process be more efficient, since the bank will already have much of your information available, but you might be able to negotiate a mortgage with more favorable terms than you might find with a different lender who is unfamiliar with your financial history. For example, a bank might offer you a discount or an incentive on your home loan if you have a checking or savings account set up through them.

The major disadvantage of using a commercial bank for your mortgage is that, again, banks do not specialize in home loans. Banks, especially the larger, nationally recognized institutions, are capable and trustworthy, but their expertise in the area of home loans might be more limited than that of other resources such as mortgage companies, which focus exclusively on home loans. Talk to the mortgage bankers at your preferred banking institution to determine whether you feel comfortable securing a home loan through your bank and to get an idea of the terms of a bank-issued mortgage for comparison with other loan sources.

Banks often require that the purchaser have a decent credit history and stable income. A bank will have strict requirements for credit history, but it is one of the most stable organizations to have your mortgage with. The price for this stability can be a higher interest rate, so shop around. If you can get preapproval from several lenders, then you can bargain more effectively for the best rate.

CREDIT UNIONS

Credit unions are similar to banks. These institutions are made up of members who belong to some defined community, such as universities, religious organizations, or government offices. Credit unions generally offer banking services, including savings and checking accounts and loans. The main difference between a credit union and a bank is that a credit union is exempt from federal taxation.

Membership in a credit union requires meeting certain parameters, but obtaining a home loan through a credit union can be extremely beneficial. Because of the tax benefits credit unions enjoy, they are often able to offer their members an easier mortgage approval process and more favorable interest rates.

Credit unions do not sell their mortgages on the secondary market. Secondary mortgage markets, which are discussed in more detail in Chapter 24, might result in reduced interest rates. However, the advantage to obtaining a mortgage through an organization that does not resell its loans on the secondary market is that you know exactly who has control over your home loan at all times. In addition, you will have to deal only with the credit union lender rather than with a third or subsequent party, as might be the case when your mortgage is traded on the secondary market.

It is worthwhile to investigate the options open to you, based on your memberships and affiliations, with respect to a credit union loan, which might prove to be easier to obtain and might offer a more attractive interest rate.

PRIVATE INDIVIDUALS

Anyone can make you a home loan — all that is required is money, willingness, and compliance with any laws on the state and federal level that dictate the terms of such loans. Regulations exist that govern even private loans, including rules pertaining to interest rates, fees and other charges, and disclosures. These regulations are primarily designed to protect you, the borrower, from what are called predatory lending practices, in which the individual loaning you money might try to take advantage of you.

With a private loan, you might not be required to obtain an appraisal or title search, but you should do so nonetheless. An appraisal will ensure that the money you are borrowing for the purchase of your home is a good reflection of what the home is worth. A title search will protect you against any future challenges to your ownership of the land you are buying.

You must refuse to sign any loan agreement that requires you to pay particularly high interest rates or has some type of penalty clause, such as a requirement that a late payment automatically entitles the lender to take your home.

Perhaps you have a friend or family member who is willing to loan you the money you need to purchase your house, maybe with very favorable terms such as little or no interest. Beware: Relationships can suffer greatly due to financial disagreements, and no matter how comfortable you feel entering into such an arrangement, know that you might be risking your money, your relationship, or both.

GOVERNMENT LOANS

In some instances, a home buyer might qualify for a loan from the government. Government loans offer many attractive features, but there are very specific requirements, and qualification is much more restricted than with other loan sources.

The Federal Housing Administration (FHA) is a federal agency under the umbrella of the United States Department of Housing and Urban Development (HUD). The FHA offers mortgage insurance on loans made to U.S. home buyers by lenders approved by the FHA. Lenders are protected by FHA mortgage insurance; in the event that the borrower defaults on the loan, the FHA covers the cost.

A major benefit of home loans insured by the FHA is that they often require a much smaller down payment than other types of loans. This makes it easier for first-time or lower-income home buyers, who are likely to have limited cash resources, to purchase a home. Qualification for a loan is easier than attempting to secure a loan from another source because lenders are more likely to trust the government to repay the money if default occurs. For the same reason, these home loans are often associated with lower interest rates than those available on the conventional mortgage market.

There are two main types of loans available to home buyers through the FHA. The first, and most commonly used, is the Fixed Rate 203(b) loan. With this type of loan, you choose the length of the period over which you will repay the loan: 15, 20, or 30 years. The shorter the length of time for repayment of the loan, the lower your interest rate will be; however, your monthly payments on the loan principal will be higher, since the total must be paid off in a shorter amount of time. A longer repayment period will result in lower monthly payments toward the loan principal, but interest rates are likely to be higher.

Regardless of the number of years for repayment of your loan, the payments and the interest will remain constant over the life of the loan. Interest rates will never increase during the time you have an outstanding balance on the loan, but they also will never decrease, even if market rates go down. Payments will be fixed, with the same amount due on the principal of the loan each month, subject only to changes in the property tax or homeowner's insurance associated with the home.

This type of loan, with its fixed payments, is a good option for home buyers who intend to stay in the same house for an extended period of time. If you plan to live in the house for at least five years and build equity in it, a fixed-rate loan is likely your best option.

A second type of FHA loan is the adjustable-rate mortgage (ARM). The interest rate associated with ARMs will be adjusted based on market interest rates. ARMs usually offer the home buyer an interest rate that is lower at the beginning of the life of the loan and rises over time; the fixed-rate period is commonly three years.

Adjustable-rate mortgages are best for home buyers who plan to live in a house for only a short, fixed time. If your plans include a probable move before the end of the fixed low-interest period at the beginning of the loan, an ARM is likely to be the option that will save you the most money.

Another government mortgage is the VA mortgage, which is backed by the Veterans Administration. To apply for a VA loan, the applicant must have served in the military. These loans are popular with first-time buyers because no down payment is required. Sometimes buyers can get assistance with closing costs as well. See Chapter 11 for more information on VA loans.

Both FHA and VA programs limit the size of the loan. This limit varies in different parts of the country. There are no income limits for applying for an FHA loan, although the focus has been to serve low- and moderate-income applicants. The FHA lenders can also be more lenient for those with poor credit.

FINANCE COMPANY MORTGAGES

Finance companies are also in the business of offering mortgages. However, you could be looking at higher interest rates. There is also the consideration that some of these companies do not have the same stability as banks.

The advantage to working with finance companies is they often deal with people who have poor credit. The banks and smaller lenders do not like to work with people with bad credit, giving the finance companies a niche market share. If you have less-than-perfect credit, check into what a finance company can do for you.

Some of these companies specialize in repairing a person's poor credit. They will work out a plan to help you improve your credit rating. There is another added advantage: Although you might start out with a higher interest rate, you can often negotiate that rate down with good payment history.

If you are having trouble because of your credit rating, consider a small mortgage lender. While not technically a finance company, a mortgage lender is also not a bank or a credit union. These companies are competitive, even for people with credit problems, because they want to build their business. However, they are small and might be relatively new compared to larger banks and other lenders, so make sure the ones you consider are reputable and stable lenders. You do not want your lender to go bankrupt in the middle of your mortgage.

THE INTERNET

With society's increasing reliance on telecommunications and constant improvements in technology, it is not surprising that a variety of options for securing a home loan exist in the virtual universe. Online resources are often more efficient and consumer-friendly, allow for easy comparison and tracking of mortgage-related data, and give a home buyer the opportunity to stay informed and be truly in control of his or her home loan.

People have become comfortable with online research, but are frequently wary of taking advantage of the Internet to secure a home loan. Many respected and recognizable institutions, such as Charles Schwab, LendingTree, Countrywide, Wells Fargo, Bank of America, and GMAC, offer online mortgage loans. When considering securing a home loan online, the most important thing is that you will have to take on full responsibility for your loan. If you are unprepared to handle all aspects of the mortgage process on your own and need a guiding presence, as many people find they do, a more conventional resource, such as a bank or credit union, might be a better option.

If you are prepared to take matters into your own hands, you will find there are many benefits to getting a mortgage online. Although guidance is limited, most online lenders offer customer service to answer any questions you might have.

Following is a step-by-step guide to using the Internet to find the best home loan available to you:

STEP 1: RESEARCH

Your first step, before considering any lenders or their offerings, should be to research prevailing mortgage rates. Many sites track interest rates and update them at least daily. They also might provide online mortgage calculators and other tools that you can take advantage of in determining how much mortgage you can afford and whether or not a particular offering is a good deal that will help you achieve your homeownership goal.

Bank Rate Monitor (**www.bankrate.com**) offers a tool where you can compare interest rates available in a particular geographical area. The Web site for the Mortgage Bankers Association of America (MBAA) at **www. mbaa.org** offers a wealth of data that includes economic forecasts, survey results, and an analysis of the market environment.

Several U.S. government sites offer helpful information. The Web site for Fannie Mae (**www.fanniemae.com**), a government-chartered, shareholder-owned company that operates in the secondary mortgage market to increase the availability of funds for home loans and offers free tools, such as a mortgage calculator, a worksheet to determine how much house you can afford, a list of government-approved lenders, a glossary, and more. Freddie Mac (**www.freddiemac.com**) is a similarly structured company, offering explanations of different types of mortgages and tools to calculate how much home you can afford and how much money you can borrow.

The HUD Web site (**www.hud.gov**) has links to both Fannie Mae and Freddie Mac and includes tools to calculate what you can afford, what the advantages and disadvantages of various types of mortgages mean for you, and other helpful information. The HUD Web site also offers detailed assistance on everything from shopping for homeowner's insurance to the process of signing papers to close on your new home.

STEP 2: SELECT A SITE

There are three main types of mortgage loan sites. The majority are direct-access sites that put you in contact with a single lender, such as a bank or other lending institution. However, in most instances these lenders have a physical presence, and you are likely to be required to contact the institution directly; complete product information is usually not available online. Most often, a bank uses its Web site to lure you into its physical building to meet with a person who can then evaluate you face-to-face and potentially try to profit from you in excess of what the institution could expect by dealing with you exclusively online.

A second type of online mortgage resource is an auction site. At an auction site, you will complete a full loan application with detailed questions pertaining to what you are looking for and your financial situation; this application is then distributed by the site to various lenders who compete for your business. Within days, and sometimes hours, you will begin to receive offers from various lenders, with terms and interest rates that can vary, sometimes significantly.

The best approach is to visit the Web site of any lender that has bid for your commitment directly to read any fine print and find out more details about the loan being offered to determine whether it is right for you. Popular and reputable loan auction sites include **www.LendingTree.com** and **www. RealEstate.com.**

If you want to secure the rates and terms offered via auction, you will likely have to respond directly to the communication you received from the lender. You might not be able to get the same deal by approaching the lender directly, so after you have done your research, work through the auction site to finalize the mortgage. The benefit of working with an auction site is that many such sites, including the aforementioned sites, offer at least limited customer service. Therefore, if you have questions or need additional guidance, you have a resource working on your behalf as an intermediary between you and the lender.

A third type of online mortgage resource is the multi-lender site. At a multi-lender site, you are not required to complete an application right away. Instead, you can shop around for a mortgage that fits your situation from among a variety of lender offerings. Popular and reputable multi-lender sites include **www.loanshop.com** and **www.eloan.com.**

Most multi-lender sites have a tool that allows you to enter information, such as details about the property you are interested in purchasing, your estimate of the amount of money required for your loan, and the approximate down payment you anticipate being able to afford. Based on this information, such a site will provide you with information about current interest rates, points, annual percentage rates (APRs), settlement costs, and more.

After you have received the information you need, you will have the option to complete an application. If you choose to do so through a multi-lender site, the site will process your application and any supplemental documents and forward the information on to the lender you have selected. However, you might be better off contacting the lender directly. Surveys have revealed that lenders sometimes treat borrowers that come to them through third-party multi-lender sites with less respect than loan seekers who approach them directly, perhaps because lenders see those that use multi-lender sites as lazy or uninformed and incapable of making a determination of the best mortgage option on their own.

STEP 3: CLOSING

If you choose to secure your mortgage online, you might decide to go through with the closing virtually as well. In most instances, home buyers and sellers, along with their real estate agents and/or attorneys, still meet face-to-face to complete a real estate closing. However, as people become more comfortable with the saving of time and money that is associated with online transactions, an increasing number of closings are occurring electronically.

Not all lenders are willing to participate in an electronic closing. Those who are willing and able to use this approach often use a closing service to facilitate the process. One popular and widely used service is ClosingStream, developed by LSI, a valuation and settlement services company. A ClosingStream representative first contacts the borrower to explain the online closing process, which usually occurs as follows:

- First, the borrower will supply personal information to the lender and answer some type of security question or series of questions to authenticate his or her identity.

- Second, the borrower will usually receive an identification code that he or she can use to access a power-of-attorney document on the ClosingStream Web site (**www.lsi.fnf.com**). Power-of-attorney means that the person signing the form (that is, you, the borrower) authorizes another party (in this case, a ClosingStream representative) to conduct the transaction on his or her behalf. The borrower must print this document out and sign it before a notary public, return the form by mail to ClosingStream, and schedule an official closing time.

- Finally, at the time of closing, the home buyer dials a number given to them by ClosingStream to participate in a conference call and simultaneously logs on to the lender's Web site. Either a title representative from the lender, or a lawyer in states where an attorney is required, will be present, and the borrower can see this individual online via Webcam images that are presented on the computer screen during the closing process.

- The closing itself usually takes under an hour, far less than most physical closings. Once the closing is complete, the pages of the closing documents that the borrower is required to sign or initial are posted online, and the borrower clicks a button on the Web page to indicate that they agree to the terms reflected therein. Ultimately, if the borrower is satisfied with all the terms and with the closing process, he or she agrees to allow ClosingStream's representative to sign the closing documents in their representative capacity.

If you go online to satisfy your mortgage needs, check all claims, research alternatives, and never commit to a transaction if you have any questions or feel skeptical about some aspect of the offer. You might come across everything from small-print tricks to bait-and-switch tactics.

If you are wary of your own ability to deal with the hurdles that are associated with taking mortgage matters into your own hands, the best option for you is to deal directly with a lender through traditional channels. If, however, you feel confident that you can spot and handle potential problems and are willing to get your hands dirty securing your own home loan, there is a wealth of information and opportunities available to you online.

MORTGAGE MARKETS & STRUCTURING

Mortgages are loans, but the structure under which they are administered is more complex than just the lending and receipt of money. There are two main mortgage markets: the primary market and the secondary market.

In the primary mortgage market, mortgage lenders deal directly with members of the public who wish to secure loans for the purchase of a home. Primary mortgage lenders originate loans, lending money directly to the borrower, and make a profit only from loan processing fees that are imposed on the loan, not from the interest paid on the loan.

Loan processing fees are intended to cover the cost of getting the paperwork together, processing the application, and issuing the mortgage. These fees vary from lender to lender. Check out the fees charged by several lending institutions in your area to make sure that what you are being charged is fair and on par with what other loan providers are charging. If you find lower rates are being charged by lenders other than the loan source you have selected, you can use this information as leverage to negotiate with your chosen lender for a lower fee or other benefits. Lenders are usually willing to compromise on some aspect of the mortgage process to ensure they keep your business.

On the primary market, there are different types of loans and different types of lenders. Some primary lenders are mortgage brokers; others are mortgage bankers. It is valuable to understand the difference:

- Mortgage bankers are also known as direct lenders. These institutions operate like banks do, lending you, the home buyer, their own money from resources amassed from fees, interest rates, and other charges. They might then retain the rights to repayment of the mortgage they have issued, with interest, or they might sell the mortgage on the secondary market, a process described in greater detail below.

- Mortgage brokers do not lend consumers their own money in the form of a mortgage. Instead, brokers are middlemen who do the work of researching various loans that are available to a potential borrower, analyzing the advantages and disadvantages of each, and bringing the borrower together with a lender that offers the most appropriate mortgage package for that particular home buyer. Often a mortgage broker will have access to a wholesale lender, a lending institution that does not deal directly with the public. Wholesale lenders might offer more attractive terms in the mortgages they offer than traditional direct lenders, so the use of a mortgage broker with such connections might pay off in your search for an affordable and appropriate mortgage. Recognize, however, that mortgage brokers will require you to pay additional fees for their services, so be certain that any extra money expended is worth your ultimate savings or other benefits of the resulting mortgage.

After your closing with your primary lender, the lender might either hold onto the mortgage or sell it on the secondary market. Currently, about half of all home loans for individual residential home purchases are traded on the secondary market. A primary mortgage lender might loan money to the borrower, then sell the mortgage note to investors on the secondary market. Mortgage notes are not sold one by one, since a single home loan is not worth enough to justify the time and effort associated with such a sale. Instead, your lender will sell your mortgage note as part of a larger package. The money the lender makes by selling such packages to secondary market investors is used to replenish the lender's cash reserves that are depleted with each loan issued, as well as to make a profit for the lender.

Who are these investors who buy mortgage notes on the secondary market? The biggest buyers are the Federal National Mortgage Association, the Federal Home Loan Mortgage Corporation, and the Government National Mortgage Association, which you have probably seen referred to as Fannie Mae, Freddie Mac, and Ginnie Mae, respectively. In addition, private financial institutions, including banks, life insurance companies, and private investors, participate in the secondary market, buying mortgage notes in the hopes of making a profit from them. The government-backed buyers tend to be the safest route for home buyers to take, particularly first-time purchasers. We will examine each in detail.

FEDERAL NATIONAL MORTGAGE ASSOCIATION

Fannie Mae is a company endorsed by the United States government through a federal charter. The company is shareholder-owned, and its mission is to ensure that lenders of mortgages that are part of Fannie Mae's nationwide network of lender partners have enough money to lend to home buyers by buying mortgage notes from the lenders on the secondary market.

The Fannie Mae Web site (**www.fanniemae.com**) offers a variety of extremely useful tools to assist you in your search for a mortgage lender, including search tools that help you figure out which type of mortgage program is best suited for your specific situation and that help you find contact information for one of the company's partner lenders in your particular state, either by name or by the type of mortgage you need.

Fannie Mae does not itself lend money directly to borrowers, but the company provides helpful guidance for those searching for information on mortgages and mortgage lenders. The Web site has a "Calculators" section to help you determine what your home and mortgage needs and restrictions are, including a "How Much House Can You Afford?" calculator.

Another resource is the "Counselors & Agencies" section of the Web site, which can help you determine whether you are equipped to handle securing a mortgage and purchasing a home on your own, or whether you should contact a housing agency or a credit counseling agency, which can work directly with you to determine if homeownership is truly right for you and, if so, how to conquer issues such as poor credit and limited funds.

The Fannie Mae Web site also offers a search tool that allows a potential home buyer to look for Fannie Mae-owned properties for sale and a glossary of real estate– and mortgage-related terms.

FEDERAL HOME LOAN MORTGAGE CORPORATION

Freddie Mac is a government-chartered company, similar to Fannie Mae, that buys mortgage notes from lending institutions, providing lenders with the money to replenish their resources and provide future loans to home buyers.

Freddie Mac funds its purchase of these mortgages mainly through securitization-based financing, whereby the company issues a security related to a mortgage or bundle of mortgages as an undivided interest to an investor or group of investors. The investors purchasing the mortgage-related security can then choose to either hold the security to realize a gradual profit over time or resell the security to other investors for immediate profit.

Freddie Mac also profits from the secondary market purchase of mortgage notes by holding some of the loans in its own retained portfolio. This money, financed through the company's issuance to investors of debt and equity securities, discussed in more detail below, is invested to make a profit for the company from the mortgages it has purchased from mortgage lenders.

For a single-family residential property, the buyer of the home sends his monthly payment on the mortgage issued to the issuing lender, who keeps a small portion as its own profit, usually referred to as a service fee, and sends the balance of the payment to Freddie Mac. Freddie Mac either retains some or all of the payment for its portfolio for reinvestment or passes some or all of the payment on to investors for a profit.

The mortgages that Freddie Mac resells to investors as securities are pooled-together groups of loans that are called mortgage-backed securities (MBS). Investors are willing to pay for these securities because Freddie Mac guarantees timely payment of principal and interest, which means that, in the event a homeowner does not pay his or her monthly mortgage payment, the investors do not suffer because Freddie Mac will pay them what they are owed and deal with the lender and the delinquent loan borrower independently. This guarantee, and Freddie Mac's outstanding reputation resulting from prompt and complete payment and government endorsement, makes investors in MBS willing to accept, as a trade-off, a slightly lower yield than that offered by other, riskier investments.

Let us look in greater detail at the two types of securities offered by Freddie Mac:

- **Mortgage-backed securities (MBS).** Freddie Mac pools together various loans, such as mortgages issued for the purchase of residential real estate, and issues MBS representing an interest in that pool of loans. The loans that are pooled together might have similar characteristics — for example, payment terms, interest rates, or length of loan repayment periods — but will also differ in some ways, including the credit history of the borrowers and the geographical location and type of property purchased with the loan money. The diversity included in these pools of mortgages helps to minimize the risk to investors. The money that investors pay to Freddie Mac for the purchase of MBS comes full circle to pay for the purchase by Freddie Mac of additional mortgage notes from primary lenders.

- **Debt securities.** Debt securities are those mortgages purchased by Freddie Mac that the company does not resell to other investors, but retains in its own portfolio for investment purposes. As with MBS, Freddie Mac receives the home buyer's monthly mortgage payment from the primary lender, less the lender's fees, but does not pass the mortgage notes on to investors. Investing the mortgages itself, Freddie Mac uses the money made to make a profit. After keeping a fee for its own purposes, Freddie Mac reinvests the money made on debt securities in primary lenders to increase lenders' ability to offer loans to mortgage-seeking home buyers.

Freddie Mac's efficient process of buying mortgages and pumping returns back into lenders' coffers allows primary lenders, who deal directly with homeowners, to always have money readily available to loan consumers who wish to purchase a home, and to be able to offer loan money to consumers promptly and at an attractive rate. Research has shown that the cash supply that primary lenders receive continually from the secondary mortgage market can drive mortgage rates down by as much as 0.5 percent, which adds up to considerable savings over the life of the mortgage.

Freddie Mac is a leader in research on mortgage markets, so the company Web site (**www.freddiemac.com**) is an excellent resource for potential home buyers researching mortgage information, including market trends, interest rates, and the like. Among the useful tools that can be found on Freddie Mac's Web site are an "Economic and Housing Outlook," updated monthly; a quarterly "Conventional Mortgage Home Price Index"; an "Adjustable-Rate Mortgage Survey," published annually; and a state-by-state evaluation of mortgage rates and the geographically specific housing market.

GOVERNMENT NATIONAL MORTGAGE ASSOCIATION

Ginnie Mae is different from Fannie Mae and Freddie Mac. Ginnie Mae does not buy or sell loans, nor does it issue MBS. Instead, Ginnie Mae guarantees investors that they will be paid in full, and in a timely fashion, on all principal and interest on MBS that are backed by loans insured or guaranteed by the federal government. In other words, investors who work with Ginnie Mae are assured payment even if the borrower of a home loan is delinquent in his or her mortgage payment.

The federally insured or federally guaranteed loans that are guaranteed by Ginnie Mae include those originating with the Federal Housing Administration (FHA), the Department of Veterans Affairs (VA), the Department of Agriculture's Rural Housing Service (RHS), and the Department of Housing and Urban Development (HUD) Office of Public and Indian Housing (PIH).

Because Ginnie Mae securities have a full faith and credit guarantee of the U.S. government, they are a safe investment, so they are attractive to investors who are risk-averse or who are willing to lower their yield expectations in exchange for minimal risk. Ginnie Mae pools eligible loans, such as those insured or guaranteed by the aforementioned government entities, and offers pro rata shares to its investors. Even when the economy faces difficult circumstances, these types of securities carry a priority of reimbursement to investors.

The securities, or pools of mortgages, that are guaranteed by Ginnie Mae fall into three main categories:

- **Ginnie Mae I MBS** are securities in which all mortgages in the pool are of the same type — for example, mortgages issued for the purchase of a single-family residential unit. Each mortgage in a given pool must be insured or guaranteed by the FHA, the VA, the RHS, or HUD's PIH, and must remain so for the lifetime of the mortgage. Each of the mortgages in the pool must have been issued by the same issuer, and the interest rates must be the same for all mortgages included in the pool. Currently, the minimum pool size for Ginnie Mae/MBS mortgage pools is $1 million total for all included mortgages.

- **Ginnie Mae II MBS** are more flexible pools of securities, allowing multiple issuers to be involved in the pool (that is, mortgages comprising the pool might have been issued by various sources). The minimum pool size for these multi-lender pools is currently $250,000 total fort all included mortgages.

- **Real Estate Mortgage Investment Conduits** (REMICs) are conduits that organize direct payments of principal and interest from underlying securities, comprised of mortgage pools, into classes. The classes are based on balances of principal, interest rates, average lifetime of the mortgages included, and other characteristics of the loans included in the security pool. REMIC payments of principal and interest do not pass to investors on a pro rata basis, but rather are divided into classes that vary in terms of their expected maturity times and amounts, among other characteristics. These REMICs allow for the offering of a variety of securities, so investors can select short-, intermediate-, or long-term maturities to fit their own personal investment needs.

Ginnie Mae offers numerous tools on its Web site (**www.ginniemae. gov**) to assist prospective home buyers in their hunt for a house and a mortgage. A set of homeownership calculators includes tools to evaluate the advantages and disadvantages for a particular individual or family of buying versus renting, to estimate how much the home buyer can afford to spend on a house, and to determine whether one is eligible for particular loans and, if so, how much money might be secured for a home purchase and with what rates and terms.

The Ginnie Mae Web site also guides users step-by-step through the home-buying process, with tools that are particularly helpful for first-time buyers. A section entitled "Homeownership 101" offers tools such as an "Are You Ready to Buy?" evaluation; a qualifications checklist; a guide to understanding tax benefits; an explanation of government loan programs; and more. Additional information is available regarding credit counseling, loan applications, the process of finding a home that is perfect for you, and a guide to the purchase itself.

Mortgages that are not insured or guaranteed by the federal government are referred to as conventional financing. Conventional financing includes all loans that come from private lenders through traditional channels — that is, mortgages that are not guaranteed by Ginnie Mae. Conventional mortgages fall into one of two categories: conforming or non-conforming:

- **Conforming loans.** Conforming loans are those that conform to the specific guidelines required by Fannie Mae or Freddie Mac. Because these loans are of low risk to the lending institution, they offer attractively low interest rates, but are also subject to strict limitations. There are three basic requirements for conforming loans:

  (i) The borrower must have a "minimum of debt." This means that your monthly expenses, including mortgage payments, property taxes, insurance, payments on other loans, and any other regular monthly charges must total no more than a specific percentage of your monthly income. This debt-to-income ratio helps to ensure you are in a financial position to pay back the money you have borrowed from the lender.

  (ii) The borrower must have a good credit rating. You will be required to be current on payments for all your outstanding debts and to meet a minimum FICO credit score.

  (iii) The borrower must have sufficient funds for closing. You will have to have enough money at your disposal to pay your down payment at closing, as well as proof of where that money came from, such as a check stub from your employer. You will also need several months worth of cash reserves that you will use to pay the initial monthly payments on your mortgage subsequent to closing, your required homeowner's insurance payments, and property tax payments.

- **Nonconforming Loans.** Nonconforming loans are more flexible and have no set guidelines that encompass all mortgages; instead, terms and requirements vary from lender to lender.

Nonconforming loans are also called "subprime" loans, to reflect that they are obtainable even by borrowers who have less-than-perfect credit scores, variable income, or other financial issues that would disqualify them from eligibility for a conforming conventional loan.

MORTGAGE PROGRAMS 101

There are many different kinds of mortgage programs available to you as a home buyer. Each has its own advantages and disadvantages, depending on your particular situation. In this chapter, we will look in depth at some of the more common types of mortgage programs so that you are well prepared to take the next step in securing a mortgage that is right for you.

FIXED-RATE MORTGAGES

The most common type of mortgage program is a fixed-rate mortgage. Fixed-rate mortgages have monthly payments, for both the principal of the loan and the interest on the loan, that never change. The total amount you pay might change slightly if there is a change in the amount of property tax due on your property or in the cost of your homeowner's insurance, but your payments should remain stable throughout the lifetime of the loan.

A fixed-rate mortgage lasts for a specific period of time, usually 15, 20, or 30 years. There might be some flexibility with your payment schedule, depending on the lender and on the amount of your loan. For example, while most fixed-rate mortgages are paid on a monthly basis, some might be paid biweekly, so that the borrower pays half the monthly amount due every two weeks.

The interest rate associated with a fixed-rate mortgage remains the same for the full life of the loan. This means that you are locked into the initial rate, so if market interest rates go down, you are stuck with the deal you signed. On the other hand, with a fixed rate, you need never worry about rising interest rates, because yours will remain steady no matter the market fluctuation.

Because of the constancy of the interest rate, a fixed-rate mortgage is most appropriate for a home buyer who intends to stay on the purchased property for an extended period of time. If you intend to live in your home for at least five years, your best course of action is likely a fixed-rate mortgage. When you are in a position to resell your home somewhere down the line, you will have built up collateral that you can use to your advantage, such as for the purchase of a subsequent home.

Payments toward principal also remain level over the loan period. The amount due each month will be calculated by the lender to ensure that, if you pay exactly that amount on each due date, you will have paid off the entire loan at the end of the term to which you committed. In the early stages of the loan repayment period, most of your monthly payment will go toward the interest owed. As you pay down your loan, the interest rate associated with it will decrease, so a larger percentage of your monthly payment will begin to be applied toward the principal of the loan.

Of course, if you pay more than is required on each due date, you will decrease the time it takes you to pay off the total. Lenders make money off the interest rates, however; therefore, some lenders might charge you a penalty fee for overpayment or for paying the full balance of the loan off before the agreed-upon term expires. Ask in advance so that you know what is expected of you. If you hope to pay off your loan early and want to avoid a penalty for doing so, you will either need to negotiate with the lender or find an alternative lender that does not penalize you for prepayment.

ADJUSTABLE-RATE MORTGAGES

Unlike fixed-rate mortgages, adjustable-rate mortgages (ARMs) have interest rates that change over time. The main benefit of an ARM is that such a loan often allows you to take advantage of attractively low interest rates. The flip side is that, by enjoying low interest rates, you take on the risk of interest rate changes. While market changes do not affect the amount of interest paid on a fixed-rate mortgage, an ARM interest rate will rise if market rates rise, and there is potential for the increase to be great. This makes ARMs with low initial interest rates a good choice for buyers who intend to stay in their home only for the short term.

Because of the risk to the borrower of the loan, ARMs have caps, or limits, on the amount by which the interest rate can change over a given period of time. Caps include limitations on how frequently an interest rate change can be implemented, the period change in the interest rate, and the total interest rate change over the entire lifetime of the loan, referred to as a life cap. For example, an interest rate cap might require interest adjustments to occur only once every six months at a maximum of 1 percent per adjustment, for a total of 2 percent interest change in one year. Lifetime caps are commonly 6 percent.

You might see the limits on adjustments associated with your loan represented as a series of numbers. Caps are sometimes expressed in the form of initial adjustment cap/subsequent adjustment cap/life cap; a cap structure of 1/2/6, for example, would indicate that your loan has a 1 percent cap on the first adjustment, a 2 percent cap on each subsequent adjustment, and a 6 percent cap on total interest rate adjustments over the lifetime of the loan.

The interest rate, and changes thereto, associated with an ARM depends on what is called an index, a rate that is set by current economic conditions (i.e., the market) and that is published by a neutral, independent source, plus a margin (or a markup) added to the index rate that represents the lender's profit for loaning you the mortgage money.

Each different index responds at a specific pace to the ups and downs of the economy, which will impact how frequently and by how much your specific interest rate changes. There are two main types of indexes. One type of index is based on rate averages; this type tends to move more gradually, with smaller effects on interest rates when the market rises or falls. The other type of index is based on spot rates; ARMs based on these types of rates rise and fall more quickly. In some instances, the two scenarios overlap.

The main benefit of an ARM that is based on rate averages is that your payment will change more slowly as the market changes. However, ARMs based on rate averages are also associated with higher margins; because the margin on such an ARM is higher, the rate you will be required to pay will also be higher. The most common indexes based on average rates are the 11th District Cost of Funds Index (COFI), which is the slowest moving and most stable of all of the indexes, and the 12-Month Moving Treasury Average (MTA), a 12-month average of the monthly average yield of relatively stable United States Treasury securities.

Commonly used indexes that are based on spot rates include the one-month LIBOR (London Interbank Offered Rate), an international index that follows the world economy rather than just the United States economy, and the Constant Maturity Treasury (CMT) index, a short-term average readjusted daily that is volatile and reacts extremely quickly to changes in the market.

We will look more carefully at the various types of indexes so that you can make a decision about the best option for you should you select an ARM to finance your home:

- **11th District Cost of Funds Index (COFI).** If you have an ARM with rates based on the COFI, your interest rate changes will be slow and gradual. Most COFI-based loans have an interest rate that is adjusted monthly and a total monthly payment, with principal and interest, that changes once per year. The main disadvantage of a COFI-based mortgage is what is called "negative amortization," which occurs when your payments over the course of a year do not cover all the interest that is due, meaning you owe more money than you borrowed in the first place. COFI-based loans are beneficial to the borrower when interest rates are rising because of the slow movement and long time before effects are felt, but not when market interest rates are falling.

- **12-Month Treasury Average (MTA).** Once a month, the United States Treasury, a Cabinet department that is also responsible for the printing and distribution of money and that houses the Internal Revenue Service (IRS), calculates the average yield on a constant-maturity one-year Treasury bill for the previous month. A Treasury bill is a short-term investment that is backed by the government, so it is safe and increases in value over the investment period (one year in the case of the one-year bill). MTA-based mortgage payments will change slowly because the rate index moves slowly, with every change in interest rate percentage being reflected in the index as 1/12th of the change every month. For example, a 1 percent increase in interest rates would cause the MTA index to go up 1/12th of 1 percent the following month, another 1/12th the subsequent month, and so on. Like the COFI, the MTA index's slow reaction to fluctuations in short-term interest rate changes smoothes the changes out so that your payments are not drastically affected all at once.

- **London Interbank Offered Rate (LIBOR).** The LIBOR index tracks the rates at which London banks borrow reserves from one another and is roughly equivalent to the federal funds rate in the United States, although it is set by the market rather than by a government entity. Therefore, the LIBOR fluctuates more quickly than either the COFI or the MTA indexes described previously. There are several different schedules associated with LIBOR maturities; the most common are one-month, six-month, and 12-month. For example, a one-month LIBOR is based on the rate for a loan of one-month duration between London banks, and the mortgage would be adjusted each month. The LIBOR is more sensitive to the world economy, rather than being limited to just fluctuations in the United States market, and the sensitivity is evident in both drops and rises in the market. With the LIBOR, the borrower shares risk with the lender.

- **Constant-Maturity Treasury (CMT).** CMT indexes follow the fluctuations in one-year United States Treasury bills on a weekly or monthly basis. Rates associated with ARMs that are based on a CMT index move up or down quickly in response to market fluctuations, and mortgages are usually adjusted once per year. CMT-indexed mortgages are, on the current mortgage market, the most popular for residential home purchasers.

There are various types of ARMs available, including convertible ARMs, hybrid ARMs, and option ARMs. We will examine each type of ARM individually:

- **Convertible ARMs.** Convertible ARMs are a combination of conventional loans and ARMs, and if you find the right convertible ARM, you might be able to get the best of both worlds.

Convertible ARMs feature the low rates that are associated with adjustable-rate mortgages, but with the option to convert your ARM to a fixed-rate conventional loan during the loan's early stages. With a convertible ARM, you can save money by getting a low mortgage rate at the outset of your loan term and benefit from a lower risk of rising interest rates. The way it works: If you think interest rates are going to rise (which, as a vigilant homeowner, you should be able to determine from your constant monitoring of the mortgage market), call your lender and ask that your interest rate be locked into the lender's current fixed-rate offering at that time. There are limits on when you can make this change; the time period might vary from lender to lender, but in most cases you can change from an ARM to a conventional loan either before closing or for a specific time immediately following closing. By utilizing a convertible loan, you can save money by avoiding the need to refinance when interest rates rise, which can be an extremely expensive proposition involving another appraisal, another title insurance payment, additional lender fees, and other costs.

- **Hybrid ARMs.** Hybrid ARMs have a fixed interest rate associated with the mortgage for a fixed period of time at the beginning of the loan period. A hybrid ARM is referred to by the initial fixed period, in years, and the adjustment periods. For example, a 3/1 ARM has a three-year initial fixed interest rate period and subsequent adjustment periods every year. The date on which a hybrid ARM changes from a fixed-rate payment schedule to an adjustable-rate payment schedule is called the "reset date"; after the reset date, your payment will depend on an index, just like any other ARM. Hybrid ARMs are extremely popular, attracting home buyers with their tantalizing initial fixed rate that assures your early years of homeownership will be free of the risks associated with a changing mortgage interest rate market.

- **Option ARMs.** An option ARM gives the borrower the option of making either a specified minimum payment at each monthly due date, an interest-only payment, or a fixed-rate payment. You might see option ARMs advertised as "pick a payment" plans or "pay-option" loans. Option ARMs are popular among home buyers because they usually have low initial interest rates and low minimum monthly payments. This translates into the ability to qualify for much larger loans than borrowers would otherwise be eligible for. This type of situation can be dangerous, however; read the fine print to make sure that you will be prepared to pay your monthly required payments once the interest rate goes up after the initial period and that you understand any penalties associated with nonpayment. An option ARM is the best choice for a home buyer whose income is sporadic. If you are self-employed, if your take-home pay varies depending on the season, or if your salary is commission-based, an option ARM might be a good choice for you because you will enjoy greater flexibility in how you pay your mortgage every month.

ARMS VERSUS FIXED-RATE MORTGAGES: WHICH IS BEST?

Even when you understand the similarities and differences of these two mortgage options, it is hard to know which way to go. Let us see if we can sort out this issue for you.

We already know that an ARM is one in which the interest rate changes after an initial period. This period can be from as short as one month to a full ten years. The shorter the schedule, the lower the interest rate will be.

For that initial time, you get to enjoy a rate that is better than most. But when that fixed period expires, an ARM can be risky for a homeowner. A 30-year fixed-rate loan, however, locks in for the life of the loan — there is no risk and no guesswork as to what the rate will be down the road.

WHEN TO GO WITH AN ARM

The consideration comes down to how long you plan on living in the house and whether you are likely to refinance.

If you are planning to sell or refinance within three to four years, it makes sense to go with a five-year ARM. You will save money because of the lower rate over the first five years, and that particular mortgage will be finished before the rate even begins to adjust.

The problem here is in anticipating how likely you are to move or refinance. Moves can be governed by events that are hard to predict. Jobs change, families split and merge, and people move for many reasons — not all of them predictable years in advance.

Refinancing also depends on many factors. If you happen to have both a first and a second mortgage, chances are you will refinance to get rid of the second loan. It will not matter if the interest rates have risen slightly — you will probably still save money by paying off that second mortgage.

This can be a good option for people who have a second mortgage or who are paying private mortgage insurance. People in this situation are more likely to refinance within the next few years.

WHEN NOT TO GO WITH AN ARM

If you have no idea how long you will be living at your new house or are planning to be there for 20 years, chances are you should go with a 30-year fixed mortgage.

Make sure that your ARM does not end up with deferred interest, also called negative amortization. In some cases, the minimum payment required is not enough to cover the interest due. With these loans, the borrower ends up owing more than he initially . This loan option was popular in the '80s when rates were high; it disappeared in the '90s, has reappeared, and is now gaining in popularity.

It is important to discuss these issues with your loan officer before making an educated decision.

INTEREST-ONLY LOANS

There has to be at least some mention of interest-only loans, if only to educate you as to what they are and how they function. Somewhere on your mortgage journey, someone will helpfully suggest that you look into "going interest only." Do not confuse this type of a loan with an option ARM.

JUST WHAT ARE THESE LOANS?

In an interest-only loan, only the interest is repaid throughout the course of the loan; the original amount is repaid at the end of the term of the loan, rolled over by the same bank, or refinanced by the owner. Normally, a loan repays something against the principal of the loan every month. This payment depends on the interest rate and the term as decided by the particular mortgage option. However, no money is paid against the principal.

WHY WOULD YOU WANT AN INTEREST-ONLY LOAN?

The interest-only loan has a lower monthly payment than a fully amortized payment, as in a regular fixed-rate mortgage. That is because the standard payment for a fixed-rate mortgage is made up of the interest payment and the principal payment.

Here is an example. In a 30-year fixed-rate mortgage of $100,000 at 6 percent, the monthly payment works out to be $599.56. With this type of mortgage, by the end of the term, the full amount borrowed will be paid back. In this first month, the payment consists of $500 in interest payments, while $99.56 is applied toward the principal. However, in the second month, the interest reduces slightly to $499.50, with a $100.06 payment against the principal. As every month goes by, the interest portion declines and the payment against the principal increases.

After five years, you will have paid out close to $36,000. Of that amount, just more than $29,000 was interest charges, while the balance was applied toward the principal.

The interest-only loan, however, will have paid the interest only; because there have been no payments toward the principal, the loan amount will never decrease, and therefore, the interest payment will never decrease. Your monthly payment, based on the above example, will be $500 for five years.

This interest-only period usually lasts from five to ten years. You have the right to pay more than the interest if you choose; however, if you cannot, you are obligated to pay only the interest payment.

WHY GO INTEREST-ONLY?

An interest-only loan might be a good option if any of the following apply to you:

You have inconsistent earnings — If you earn a salary that is inconsistent from month to month, this type of loan gives you payment flexibility. If one month you have an exceptional month, then you can pay a larger payment, putting more against the principal. If you have months when your cash flow is low, then you are not locked into the higher payment.

An example is someone who earns a stable, steady paycheck but receives large bonuses once or twice a year.

You want to qualify for a larger mortgage — If you want to buy a larger home and you cannot because of your income, this loan option lowers the monthly payment, therefore raising the loan amount you can qualify for.

You want to pay off high-interest loans — If you are making high-interest payments on a second mortgage, it makes sense to limit your payments, free up more cash, and pay down the higher loan.

Your cash is strapped in the short term — If you have a low cash flow in the short term, but know that within a year or two you are going to be in different circumstances, this can be a good option for you.

THE NEGATIVES OF INTEREST-ONLY LOANS

Not all loans have interest-only options. You need to talk to your loan officer and listen to his suggestions.

There is strong debate about interest-only loans; let us take a look at why you might not want to take on this type of loan.

You do not build equity — This is probably the biggest negative for this loan option. As you are not required to pay down any principal, you are not building any equity in the house. The balance you started with will be the same balance five years later if you are not making extra payments specifically against the principal.

In the first five years of a fixed-rate mortgage, you do not build much equity because the payments are almost all interest. However, you do build some. If that little bit of equity is better being utilized on a monthly basis in your day-to-day living, then still consider the interest-only option.

You're hit with higher rates — It is possible that you will be charged a higher rate for this loan option because the chances of default on this loan are higher than on a loan that amortizes. This rate difference can run about a quarter point higher.

NICHE LOANS

These loans cater to specific niche areas, like environmentally conscious buyers — people who like the idea of living close to their method of transportation or who want to buy a house with energy-efficiency features.

Countrywide is one of several vendors that offer "energy-efficient mortgages," intended for people who want to buy houses that meet a high energy-efficiency standard set by the U.S. Environmental Protection Agency. These mortgages have a standard interest rate, but allow buyers to buy more-expensive homes. The expected lower utility bills are factored into the costs of ownership.

There is also a mortgage option called the "location-efficient mortgage." These mortgages, offered by lenders as a pilot program, are for buyers who want to be close to public transportation in Los Angeles, the San Francisco Bay Area, and Seattle. In these cases, the credit ratios are adjusted to enable borrowers to buy more than they would be able to otherwise. Future lower transportation costs are added into the calculations to increase the buyer's overall income.

Clearly, there are many options. It is important to research all of them to choose the best one for you.

VA LOANS

In 1944, Congress passed a bill called the Serviceman's Readjustment Act, more commonly called the G.I. Bill of Rights. This bill was created to help veterans readjust to civilian life by offering them low-interest loans, as well as bonuses and medical benefits. One of the sections of this bill guaranteed home loans to eligible veterans. The credit standards and guidelines were still strictly followed to protect the veterans from taking on mortgage debts that they would not be able to honor. As of 2006, the VA will guarantee a maximum of 25 percent of a home loan amount up to $104,250. That sets the maximum loan amount at $417,000 with no down payment.

These guaranteed loans are made by banks, savings and loans, or mortgage companies to eligible veterans. It is this guarantee that gives the lender the protection that would have come from a down payment.

These loans are some of the most successful on the market today. Some lenders specialize, process high volumes of these loans, and will have up-to-date knowledge of the underwriting distinctions. If you are a veteran, look for a lender that knows these loans and can help you qualify for one.

FEATURES OF VA LOANS

There are several distinctive features to these loans:

- There is usually no down payment requirement unless the purchase price is greater than the VA appraisal. This appraisal is also called the Certificate of Reasonable Value (CRV). There is also a chance that, depending on the borrower's qualifications, the lender might require some money down to make the loan.

- A veteran can own more than one property through VA loans.

- Loan rates are competitive or below market rate when compared against conventional fixed-rate loans.

- A seller can help a buyer in paying the closing costs.

VA LOAN CLOSING COSTS

The veteran can pay for all reasonable and normal amounts for the itemized fees and charges as defined by VA, plus a 1 percent flat fee from the lender and reasonable discount points. Some areas, like construction and home repair loans, have special provisions.

MINIMIZING VA CLOSING COSTS

Many veterans are under the misunderstanding that all closing costs are covered by the VA loan.

This is not true; however, there are things you can do to minimize or eliminate the closing costs. One way to do this is to increase the purchase price and have a written clause stating that the seller will pay the closing costs and prepaid expenses in equal value to the amount that you increased the price. This works as long as the home appraisal is as high as the increased price. Then you will have the closing costs paid as part of the deal. There can be as high as a 3 to 5 percent difference in closing costs and prepaid expenses. It helps to understand just what these are.

VA ITEMIZED FEES AND CHARGES

The VA defines the allowable fees that the veteran borrower can pay and the closing costs that can be charged to the veteran borrowed. Any other costs in the transaction are not allowed and must be paid by the seller when the veteran borrower is purchasing a new home, or by the seller when the veteran borrower is refinancing his current VA mortgage.

The VA itemized fees and charges that the veteran borrower can pay are:

- Appraisal and compliance inspections: The veteran can pay the VA appraiser and VA compliance fees. The veteran can pay for a second appraisal, but only if they are asking for a reconsideration of value. They cannot pay for a second appraisal if the lender or the seller wants a reconsideration of value.

- Recording fees and taxes.

- Credit report, if obtained by lender.

- Items that are prepaid: This includes a portion of taxes, assessments, and other items that are chargeable to the borrower. The veteran can also pay the initial deposit for the tax and insurance account.

- Hazard insurance, including flood insurance.

- Flood zone determination: This is the determination of whether the property is in a special flood-hazard zone and must be completed by a third party who guarantees the accuracy of their results.

- Survey: The veteran can pay the survey fee if it is required by the lender.

- Title examination and title insurance.

- VA funding fee: Each veteran must pay a funding fee to the VA unless they are exempt.

- Other authorized fees: Other fees require VA authorization. The lender can request approval for the specific fee it is normally paid by any other borrowers in the particular region if it is considered normal and reasonable.

Fees that cannot be charge to the veteran's itemized fees and charges have to be covered by the lender from its 1 percent fee. These charges include:

- Closing fees
- Documentation fees
- Loan preparation fees
- Conveyance fees
- Application fees
- Interest rate lock-in fees
- Notary fees
- Membership or entrance fees
- Tax service fees
- Postage charges
- Stationery
- Amortization schedules
- Processing fees
- Loan broker's fees
- Escrow charges
- Trustee's fees
- Telephone calls
- Finders' fees

Some of these can be negotiated as part of the deal with the seller. Consult the realtor handling your transaction for advice.

APPLICATION CHECKLIST

Here is a list to make sure you have collected all the pieces that are required for your loan application:

1. Social Security number

2. Home addresses for the past two years

3. Employment information for the past two years

4. Current salary information

5. A list of all your bank accounts showing names, locations, types, and balances

6. Loan information with names, locations, accounts, balances, and payments

7. Information on other real estate you own

8. Estimate of personal property

9. Certificate of Eligibility and DD214

10. W2s for the past two years and current check stubs

11. If you are self-employed, you need to provide two years of personal income returns, current income statement, and balance sheet for the business

You will also need to pay for the property appraisal and credit report.

OCCUPANCY LAW

U.S. law requires that a veteran who obtains a VA-guaranteed loan must certify that they intend to occupy the property as their primary residence. As of the certification date, the veteran must live on the property or intend to move in within 60 days after the loan closing.

This applies to VA-guaranteed loans but not to interest rate reduction refinancing loans. For these loans, the veteran needs to certify that he previously made his home on the property.

THE RULES ON COSIGNERS OR JOINT VA LOANS

The VA rules recognize legally married spouses of veterans as cosigners on VA loans. This means their income can be included in the application. These loans are still fully guaranteed by the VA.

The guidelines also allow for more than one veteran to purchase a home together. VA divides the entitlement charge equally between them, if possible. These loans are also fully guaranteed by the VA.

If a nonveteran nonspouse wishes to cosign a loan, the VA will allow it, but will not fully guarantee the loan. The VA guarantee is limited to only the veteran's interest in the property.

WHO IS ELIGIBLE FOR A VA LOAN?

To obtain a VA loan, you have to have a VA Certificate of Eligibility.

Eligibility means you served active duty in the Army, Navy, Air Force, Marine Corps, or Coast Guard and were honorably discharged after 90 days or more, and part of the time was during wartime, or you have served 181 continuous days or more during peacetime.

TWO-YEAR REQUIREMENT

If you either:

- Enlisted after September 7, 1980

Or

- Were an officer and service began after October 16, 1981

You must have completed either:

- 24 months or more

Or

- The full period when ordered to active duty, but not less than 90 days during wartime or 181 continuous days in peacetime

There are other situations in which you might be eligible. If you either:

- Were discharged with a service-connected disability, or

- Were discharged after completing at least 20 months of a two-year enlistment, or

- Completed not less than 90 days, any part of which was during wartime, or 181 continuous days at peacetime, and one of the following conditions apply:

  o You were discharged because of a hardship, or

  o You have a service-connected, compensable disability, or

  o You were discharged or released from active duty for a medical condition which preexisted service and is not service-connected, or

  o You received a discharge or release from active duty as a result of a reduction in force, or

  o You were released from active duty for a physical or mental condition that is not classed as a disability and is not the result of misconduct but which did interfere with your ability to perform on the job

- Are the spouse of a veteran who died while in service or from a service-connected disability, and you remain unmarried

Or

- Are a spouse of a serviceperson missing in action or a prisoner of war

ACTIVE DUTY

For those of you who are on active duty now, you are eligible after serving 90 continuous days. For those without wartime experience, a minimum of 181 days of continuous active duty is required.

SIX-YEAR REQUIREMENT

A veteran who is not eligible, but who completes six years as a member of the Selected Reserve, is eligible if he:

- Received an honorable discharge

- Has been placed on the retired list

- Was transferred to the Standby Reserve after honorable service in the Selected Reserve

- Remains part of the Selected Reserve

The six years served does not have to be continuous or in the same unit. Active-duty regular military service cannot be added to Reserve service to reach the six-year requirement.

Eligibility is possible for:

1. United States citizens who served in the armed forces of a government allied with the United States in World War II

2. Individuals who served as members in organizations, like Public Health Service officers, officers of the National Oceanic and Atmospheric Administration, and merchant seamen with WWII service.

MORTGAGE LENDERS & HOW TO CHOOSE

With so many resources out there for obtaining a mortgage loan, you might wonder how to know whether a mortgage lender meets your needs and whether they will continue to do so to your satisfaction throughout your relationship. Buying a house, and getting the money to do so, is a huge endeavor. In this chapter, we will help guide you to the right mortgage lender for you, so that you can feel secure in the knowledge that the lender on whom you are depending for your new home purchase is reliable and a perfect fit.

One obvious consideration in selecting a lender is the interest rate being offered. A low interest rate is always attractive, but dig deeper and read any fine print. Low rate offerings might be associated with other, less tantalizing terms, especially if your credit is less than perfect.

Research a variety of lenders and what they have to offer, looking beyond the numerical interest rate offered. For example, do you have friends or family who recently have purchased a home or refinanced on an existing home? If so, ask them about their experience with their lender; were they satisfied with the process? Do they think the relationship they have established with the lender is valuable? Would they work with the lender again?

If you are working with a real estate agent, ask him or her for recommendations. Take suggestions from a real estate broker with a grain of salt, however, as some people in the real estate field are affiliated with specific lending institutions and might be biased. This is a valuable source of information, though, because real estate agents know the market and the process of obtaining a mortgage from their work in the field. In addition, real estate agents depend on the sale and purchase of real estate for their livelihood, so it is always in their best interest to match you up with a lender who can make purchasing a home possible for you.

What should you look at to determine whether a particular lender is the right source of a mortgage for you? First, if you decide to use a traditional lender rather than a private individual or other alternative source of funds, ensure that the lender is a Certified Mortgage Broker. Certified Mortgage Broker is a designation bestowed upon qualified lenders by the National Association of Mortgage Brokers (NAMB). The NAMB certifies mortgage brokers who meet rigorous standards, so you can be sure that a Certified Mortgage Broker is educated, competent, and ethically prepared to handle your particular mortgagee needs. Certified Mortgage Brokers are trained and certified in all aspects of mortgage lending, so they are the best resource to provide you with top-quality service during the home-buying process.

Next, research lenders. Telephone prospective lenders or visit their Web sites to find out about the various types of mortgages they offer, which ones you personally might qualify for, mortgage terms, fees, interest rates, escrow terms, closing requirements, loan servicing, and any other credit information you might need to make an educated decision about which loan option is the best one for you. If you do your research online or find out information about a particular lender through a third party, it is in your best interest to contact the lender directly, either in person or by telephone. There might be hidden terms that can be important to your ultimate decision regarding a lender that might not be obvious until you deal directly with a representative of the lending institution.

If a lender cannot or will not answer your questions, move on. You do not want to go into this major decision without the maximum amount of information available, and a qualified lender should be willing to guide you. Remember, requesting information never obligates you in any way. If you feel pressured, find another lender to deal with. How a lender's representatives treat you before you sign on to secure a mortgage through them is a good indication of the sort of treatment you are likely to get throughout the process of obtaining a mortgage, purchasing a home, and onward, for as long as you deal with the lender. If you feel skeptical or uncomfortable, do not settle.

A mortgage lender is ultimately in service to you. As you conduct your research, lenders that are worth your consideration will be those who do not pressure you but who are willing to provide you with all information you need and any additional information that you simply want to know, including things like hidden costs that might be less attractive than that low interest rate the lender advertises.

If you find a lender that looks promising, check out the history of the company on the Internet or at your local library. Find out everything you can about the lender's reputation, either online; from friends, family, colleagues, or acquaintances that have dealt directly with the lender or are familiar with the lender's reputation; from your real estate agent, real estate attorney, or anyone else in the field who is in a position to know something about the lender; or by contacting an organization such as the National Association of Mortgage Brokers (discussed above and with an online presence at **www.namb.org**) or your local Better Business Bureau (BBB; find contact information at **www.bbb.org**).

There are some warning signs that you should be aware of as you investigate your mortgage options. One red flag is a lender who refuses to quote you a specific interest rate or who is vague about its service terms or costs and fees. Also, be wary of any lenders that solicit your business through e-mail or through direct mailings, often offering particularly low interest rates; these types of offers are almost always associated with problematic terms that can harm your credit, increase your debt, or worse. Also, avoid lenders who claim you are already prequalified for a loan; there should be at least some background information divulged by you before a lender can make an honest evaluation of whether or not you are likely to be eligible for a loan from them.

Here is a good process for finding a lender who suits your needs in your quest for an appropriate mortgage:

- **Make a list.** Talk to people you know and trust about their mortgage lenders. Read the real estate or business section of your local newspaper. Check online and ensure mortgage brokers you are considering and including on your list are Certified Mortgage Brokers according to the NAMB.

- **Talk to representatives.** Loan officers or other representatives of lending institutions should be able to answer your questions honestly, completely, and clearly without making you feel pressured. A telephone call or, even better, a face-to-face visit, will give you a feel, not only for how comfortable you are with the options the lender has to offer in terms of a mortgage for you, but also how comfortable you would personally be working with the lender and its employees based on whether they respect you and how they approach your needs.

- **Get references.** You can ask the lender directly for references; feel free to contact these references and ask as many questions as you feel necessary to make an informed decision — these are people who have agreed to be contacted in this capacity and, because they are not employed by the lender, are likely to give you honest information about their own experiences working with the lender. Also seek out independent information from sources such as people in the real estate field, the Internet, or your own acquaintances who might have some inside information on a given lender.

- **Compare rates for similar loans.** Interest rates can vary widely depending on the type of loan; how much of a down payment you will be making; the length of time for repayment of the loan; whether the loan is a fixed-rate loan, an ARM, some alternative financing scheme, or a combination of any of those; and many other considerations. When you compare the rates offered by various lenders, make sure that you are comparing similar loans to ensure an accurate depiction of what you can expect for a particular set of circumstances. Besides interest rates, also look at the other terms of each lender's offerings, including costs and fees, approach to customer service, and the like. There might be a trade-off; for example, you might be in a position where it makes sense to take on a slightly higher interest rate in exchange for a lower required down payment.

Finally, consider carefully how you feel personally about a lender and its representatives; in other words, do you "mesh"? A good lender should make you feel comfortable enough to ask questions that give you the maximum possible amount of information. Communication is key. A lender should:

- **Offer proper disclosures.** Your lender should freely provide you with a good-faith estimate of your prospective interest; a truth-in-lending disclosure, required by federal law to give you complete information about the costs of your mortgage so you can make an informed comparison with the costs associated with other sources of mortgage loans; and a mortgage loan origination disclosure. All these are initial disclosures that must be sent to you within three days of the date when a lender accesses your credit report.

- **Communicate effectively.** The lender should return your telephone calls and e-mail communications promptly and certainly within the time period in which they promise to do so. This is a sign of respect and appreciation of your business by the lender.

- **Inform you of changes.** If an interest rate changes or if there are any other changes in the terms of your promised loan since the initial disclosures were made, no matter how minor, the lender should notify you and redisclose all information as soon as possible and certainly within three days before your closing at the latest.

YOUR FINANCIAL INFORMATION

CREDIT BUREAUS AND THE SCORING SYSTEM

One of the main things a mortgage lender will look at in determining whether you qualify for a loan and, if so, how much money you are entitled to, is your credit report. A borrower's credit history is important to lenders for obvious reasons: If you have a good reputation for paying back debts fully and in a timely fashion, you are likely to do the same with a home mortgage issued to you by the lender. On the other hand, if your credit history shows massive debt, delinquency in payments, bankruptcy, and similar problems, a lender will be less likely to want to risk loaning you money for a home purchase.

Credit reports put together a wide variety of financial information, including how you pay your bills, how you repay debts, how much credit you have available, what your monthly expenses are, and a wide variety of other information that reflects on your financial situation. A credit report does not state whether you are a good credit risk, a bad credit risk, or somewhere in between, but it does provide potential lenders with the information they need to make their own decision, based on their own criteria, regarding whether or not to issue you a mortgage.

The information reflected in your credit report is collected from people and entities with which you have financial dealings — for example, merchants, your landlord, and other lenders who have loaned you money. The information is collected and compiled into the report by credit bureaus, also called credit reporting agencies. Credit bureaus obtain all the relevant information and then sell your credit report to businesses, such as the entity from which you hope to secure a mortgage, so that the purchasers of the credit report can evaluate you for eligibility after you have applied for credit with them.

There are more than 1,000 credit bureaus in the United States, most of them local or regional bureaus that can get the information reflected in your credit report directly from those with whom you do business. These smaller credit bureaus are affiliated with one of three large, national credit bureaus: Equifax, Experian, and TransUnion, described in greater detail below. These large national bureaus are the entities that ultimately put together all relevant information about you into comprehensive reports on which mortgage lenders rely.

Although larger creditors report all their financial activity with you to each of the "big three" credit reporting bureaus, smaller creditors might only deal with one of the entities, so it is in your best interest to obtain copies of your own credit report from each of the three and compare them for any anomalies. All U.S. residents are entitled to a free copy once per year from each of the big three. Let us briefly look at each of these credit bureaus:

- **Equifax.** Equifax provides prompt, accurate, and complete information to potential lenders on the credit status and history of a loan applicant. In addition, Equifax offers a broad range of services for individual consumers, which you might find helpful. Some of the tools offered by Equifax on its Web site (**www.equifax.com**) include "Score Watch," which allows you to find out how you can achieve your ideal credit score and to see what kind of interest rate you can expect from lenders given your credit report; track your credit score over time as you make changes and accrue debt, data that allows you to search for the rates offered by various lenders; and compare yourself to credit averages in your local area and nationwide. The Web site also has resources to help you understand why your credit score is what it is. You can request a free copy of your credit report from Equifax through the company's Web site, by calling Equifax at (800) 685-1111, or by writing to the company at Equifax Credit Information Services, Inc., P.O. Box 740241, Atlanta, GA 30374.

- **Experian.** Experian offers a variety of tools for lenders to use when dealing with borrowers' credit information, including tracking tools to assist in tracking down hard-to-find debtors, filters to categorize customers by the type of debt or debts they owe, and a prioritization program that organizes creditors in order of how likely they are to repay their debt. Clearly, nearly everything about your credit history, both good and bad, will come to light for potential lenders using these services, so you should get a copy of your credit report well in advance of beginning your hunt for a mortgage lender and, if necessary, take steps to resolve anything that a lender might view as a red flag. You can get a free copy of your credit report from Experian online (**www.experian.com**), by calling Experian at (888) EXPERIAN (888-397-3742), or by writing to the company at P.O. Box 2104, Allen, TX 75013.

- **TransUnion**. TransUnion maintains a database that includes information gathered from more than 85,000 entities that grant credit to consumers, which is updated and audited regularly to ensure current and comprehensive information. TransUnion credit reports include identifying information on specific consumers, a complete credit history, any inquiries issued with respect to the consumer, and information gathered for public records, such as bankruptcy filings. Additional options provided by the reporting bureau include models that help lenders predict your future credit behavior based on your past and current credit profile, and credit summaries that narrow your credit information down for the lender based on the specific areas of interest, such as income or outstanding debt. You can request a free credit report from TransUnion through the company Web site (**www.transunion.com**), by calling the company at (800) 916-8800, or by sending a written request to P.O. Box 1000, Chester, PA 19022.

You can get a copy of your credit report from each of the three aforementioned credit bureaus all at once. Each of the three companies' Web sites provides you with the ability to order not just that entity's version of your credit report but those of the other two as well. Additional resources for obtaining all three versions of your credit report include the Web site **www.freecreditreport.com**, which also allows you to view your credit reports online, and the United States Federal Trade Commission, the government entity that regulates credit bureaus and protects consumers, from which you can request your credit report and other information through its Web site (**www.ftc.gov**), by telephone at (877) 322-8228, or by mailing your request to Annual Credit Report Request Service, P.O. Box 105281, Atlanta, GA 30348-5281.

Once a lender obtains your credit report, how is the report interpreted and what does it mean for your ability to obtain a mortgage? Lending institutions hire professionals to analyze your credit report and determine whether or not you are eligible for a loan, and if so, what the maximum amount they can offer to loan you should be. There might be information in your credit report that does not seem problematic to you, but which lenders might interpret negatively. Following is a brief discussion of potential red flags on your credit report that might make a lender wary of issuing you a mortgage:

- **Inquiries.** There are two types of inquiries: "hard inquiries" and "soft inquiries." Credit card applications, for example, are hard inquiries. Whether or not you are actually issued the credit card for which you have applied, and regardless of whether or how much you actually use the credit card, potential lenders might view such inquiries either as evidence that your financial situation is such that you need additional credit or that you are willing to take on additional debt; both situations make you a high credit risk and limit the amount of money you are likely to be issued in the form of a mortgage. Soft inquiries do not show up on the credit report that potential lenders see; these inquiries include things like your own or your employer's requests to view your credit report. How much should you worry about the appearance and effect of hard inquiries? A good rule of thumb is that any more than six credit card inquiries within six months' time will likely label you as a risky credit applicant. Inquiries older than six months are generally less of a problem; most inquiries are dropped from your credit report altogether after two years.

- **Open credit accounts.** Open credit accounts are any accounts considered open, even if they are not active. For example, you might have credit cards for department stores or specialty use that you use rarely or never and that you might have forgotten about altogether. They are still open accounts and signal to potential lenders that you are in a position to ring up potentially serious debt through the readily available credit, even if you intend nothing of the sort. The best remedy for this scenario is to close the accounts that you never use. However, note that experts from the big three credit bureaus do suggest keeping open your oldest credit card account because it has the most history and allows a lender or anyone else investigating your credit report to see that you have some sort of financial track record.

- **Missed payments.** Your payment history on outstanding debts is one of the most obvious things potential lenders look at. You should always avoid default, even if it means making only the minimum payment; alternatively, look into consolidation options, available by contacting your creditors directly, which might help reduce your payments and get you back on track. Flat-out delinquency — missing payments altogether — especially for several payment periods in a row, is the worst thing you can do for your credit. Delinquencies continue to appear on your credit report for seven years, even if you catch up on your payments.

- **Maxed-out lines of credit.** Maxed-out credit cards and other lines of credit are another red flag to potential lenders. Spending the maximum amount of credit available to you signals that you are either financially strapped or irresponsible with your monetary resources. The best way to avoid what might be a real problem in securing a home mortgage is not to max out your credit lines in the first place. Alternatively, move some of your debt around; in other words, contact your creditors on the maxed-out lines of credit and transfer some of the debt to other, nonmaxed out credit cards. This spreading of debt, although not ideal, is less of a red flag to future lenders than any lines of credit that are strained to the absolute maximum.

- **Debt-to-income ratio.** Lenders use the ratio of your debt owed as reflected in your credit report to the amount of income you bring in to determine how solvent you are and, consequently, how likely you are to be able to meet your monthly mortgage payments. A good threshold to keep in mind is that you should keep your unsecured debt (that is, any debt that is not tied to property, such as credit card debt) to less than 20 percent of your total income. Home and car loans are considered secured debt and are more acceptable to lenders when considering your credit worthiness.

One of the most important parts of your credit report is your credit score. A credit score is a number, calculated by the bureau issuing the report, based on your credit history. The credit score is a simple, succinct way of reflecting your credit status to a potential lender to assist them in deciding whether or not to issue you a mortgage. The credit score is calculated by assigning points to the information included in the full credit report. The numerical credit score is also a simple way for lenders to compare your credit to that of other consumers, thereby predicting how likely you are to repay the loan and make your required payments on time.

There are actually several different methods of calculating a credit score. The most common is called a FICO, which originated with an independent company, Fair Isaac and Company, that came up with the original scoring method and developed the credit report interpretation software that is currently used by banks and other lending institutions, as well as insurance companies and other businesses. Each of the big three national credit unions — Equifax, Experian, and TransUnion — has its own version of the FICO score, but each is based on the original method and provides the same numerical results for a given credit report. Some lenders also have their own scoring methods that they might use in place of or in addition to the credit score provided by a credit bureau.

Your credit score will fall somewhere in the numerical range of 300 to 900. The national average credit score is 677. A score above 700 is considered great credit; anything above 720 is deemed outstanding. A score below 660 is considered less-than-great; anything below 620 will make buying a home challenging; and anything below 580 will make it difficult.

Thirty-five percent of the score comes from your payment history: whether you pay debts off completely, at the minimum required on each payment due date, or with delinquency in your payment past.

Another 30 percent of the score comes from any outstanding debt reflected in your credit report, including money owed on car loans, home loans, and credit cards. Because credit cards are unsecured debt, they are evaluated with especially close scrutiny by lenders; the more credit cards you have with a high amount owed, especially if any or all of them are maxed out, the lower your score will be.

An additional 15 percent of your score is dependent on how long you have had credit. The longer your credit history is, the better your overall score might be because more information about your past payment history provides lenders with a more complete history of your credit habits and a more accurate prediction of your probable future credit actions.

Another 10 percent of your score falls into a category that Fair Issac calls, "New Credit." This category is simply as it says. Any new credit your apply for is calculated into your credit score under this category. The principle behind this category is that if you are searching for new credit, then you will be a greater credit risk. The more new credit you have on your account, the more adversely your credit will be effected.

The final 10 percent of your credit score is based on the number of inquiries present on your credit report. Many inquiries, accrued by your application for credit cards and loans, will be bad for your credit score. The more inquiries you have, the more likely it is, in the view of a potential lender, that you might be in financial trouble and need to obtain extra resources or that you are fiscally irresponsible. This is true even if you do not ultimately use the cards you have applied for or do not take advantage of a loan for which you have been approved. Make sure that you stay aware of all your applications and all your open credit accounts and eliminate those you do not need or use to avoid the bad reflection on you as a credit risk.

Your credit score will signal to potential lenders whether you should be offered any sort of loan. Even if you are approved for a mortgage, your credit score will affect how much money you actually receive. The higher your credit score is, the less risky you are viewed to be as a borrower, which is likely to increase the size of the mortgage you qualify for.

Let us say you have diligently ordered your free annual credit report from each of the big three reporting bureaus and are ready to take the necessary steps to improve your credit report and credit score so that once you start applying for mortgages, potential lenders will not hesitate to fund your new home purchase. Do you have some less-than-perfect items in your credit history? Do not despair. There are ways to improve your credit:

- **Check for errors.** We all know the saying "Nobody's perfect." Even established, national entities that millions of people and the national economy rely on, like Equifax, Experian, and TransUnion, are not immune to human error, technological problems, and other issues. When you receive your credit report, check it carefully to make sure there is nothing on it that is a mistake. If you are suspicious about some activity on the report, contact the issuing bureau or the Federal Trade Commission (FTC) immediately. There could be an accidental error, or you might be a victim of fraud or identity theft. Either way, it is imperative that you get any mistakes or fraudulent activity taken care of as soon as possible, while the source of the error or fraud is still traceable. You might find that what made your credit score disturbingly low was something that was not related to your actual financial activity.

- **Improve your debt-to-income ratio.** Potential lenders look very closely at this ratio, so keep the amount you owe on your credit cards and other lines of credit as low as possible. Keep your debt to less than 20 percent of your annual income.

- **Keep old lines of credit.** Lenders like to see that you have maintained some credit for a long time, which not only provides a more complete and accurate picture of your credit habits, but also indicates your willingness to stick with a particular creditor and your responsibility in maintaining a specific source of credit.

- **Reduce credit card balances.** Most financial experts suggest that you make the best impression on potential lenders by keeping your unsecured credit card debt below 25 percent of the maximum credit available on a particular card. Of course, this number might be an unrealistically low level for some mortgage applicants to achieve; in any case, keep the outstanding debt as low as possible and certainly at or below 75 percent of the total available credit. Again, this might require redistribution of your debt among your various lines of credit.

- **Avoid inquiries.** The more inquiries there are on your credit report, the lower your score, so avoid allowing inquiries unless they are absolutely necessary.

- **Pay on time.** This suggestion seems obvious and is usually easier said than done. Nevertheless, paying your debts on time is the most important thing you can do to increase your credit score and assure potential lenders that you are reliable and worthy of issuance of a mortgage.

ERRORS ON YOUR CREDIT REPORT

It is important to check your credit history for accuracy. Sometimes bank accounts show as being open and overdue when they are actually closed. If there are mistakes of any kind, get them cleared up.

There are several ways to formally dispute an error on your credit report. First, download and fill out the consumer dispute form for whatever agency has incorrectly reported your credit information. The agency must investigate the complaint and report their findings to you within a certain amount of time.

If you do not receive a satisfactory answer, contact the creditor directly. Often, it is best to do both at the same time to coordinate your efforts with all involved. If the error is ultimately corrected, the credit-reporting agency must send a report with the corrected item included to all entities that received the report with the error.

If after all this you still have not received the answer that you are looking for, you have the opportunity to put a comment on your report explaining the situation, which can be renewed every six months to stay on the report. While this is likely not that satisfying, it will at least explain the situation to potential lenders during the time that you explore options. The last resort is to contact an attorney to see what your rights are and to possibly litigate the issue.

BUYING WITH BAD CREDIT

Buying a house with bad credit can be tough, but it is not impossible.

Unfortunately, personal debt loads and bankruptcy rates are on the rise. If you have had to file for bankruptcy in the past, it stays on your credit for ten years. This can significantly lower your credit score. Anything you can do to avoid declaring bankruptcy is usually the best option. You might need the services of a credit-counseling agency. You need to research these agencies to find a reputable one that can help you in your specific situation.

Part of the problem with having poor credit is that you likely are strapped for cash or you would not be in this situation in the first place. This means you will not likely have a large down payment to use; you might need a second mortgage, as you will have to have 100 percent financing for your home.

Right now, interest rates are at record lows. With bad credit, you will not be able to get as good an interest rate as if you had wonderful credit. However, you will still get a reasonable rate in today's market. If you do need a second mortgage, the mortgage rate for that mortgage will be higher. The two rates together can create heavy payments. Can you afford it? Is it a good idea?

The best way to answer these questions is to look at the property. Is it a good investment? Can you handle the payments without getting into debt down the road? Would you survive another financial crisis?

You have options.

If you decide to move ahead and try to purchase a house with your bad credit rating, be aware of what is called a bad credit mortgage.

A bad credit mortgage is a mortgage that gives you a chance to establish good credit. If you already have a mortgage, this can be used for refinancing as well. It can also be a good thing if you do not have any credit. If you have never had a loan, you will have a low credit rating.

A bad credit mortgage can give you the opportunity to:

- Establish or clean up your credit

- Get some relief from high-interest debt

- Consolidate existing bills into one monthly payment

- Get relief from current creditors by paying them off

- Get extra cash for extensive home repairs or emergencies

- Leverage yourself out of a possible bankruptcy

You will need to work with a lender in this situation.

Alternatively, if you think your personal situation will improve over the next few years, allowing you to clean up your credit record, you might want to consider waiting. You will have a chance to save money for a down payment and will qualify for a better rate. Also consider that the amount of money you would be paying on higher-interest and second-mortgage loans could be saved for the down payment in the future.

Get some financial advice. This situation needs to be looked at carefully. Do not jump into a new situation that will make your life worse down the road.

A MORTGAGE AFTER BANKRUPTCY

It is possible to have good credit after bankruptcy. The first thing to do is to rebuild and repair your credit, as your credit score will be extremely low after declaring bankruptcy. The best way to increase your score again is to get more credit. It is relatively easy to get credit right after declaring bankruptcy. But it helps to know how to do so, and applying for a mortgage is not the easiest place to start.

There are lenders that will set you up with a secured credit card. This is where you put money into an account to guarantee the amount owed on your card; the spending limit is equal to the money you have set aside as a guarantee. The interest rate is higher for these types of cards. Use the card on a regular basis but always pay off the balance on time. In this way, you will quickly improve your credit rating.

You can get these cards with no application fee and a reasonably low annual fee. After a year, try to convert your secured card over to an unsecured card. If you have a good payment history, this should be no problem.

Another way to recover from the stigma of bankruptcy is to start saving. Opening and paying into a simple savings plan on a regular basis will also help to repair your credit score. You can also apply for an "installment loan." You will have to pay high interest at the beginning if you buy a new vehicle. However, you can trade it in early, and with a good payment history, you will be able to get a second vehicle at a much better interest rate.

Once you have done some credit repair, it is easier to apply for a mortgage. This credit repair can be with secure cards, regular utility payments, and installment loans. Find a loan officer who will work with your history. You will pay a higher rate and higher fees, so to minimize this, save as much as you can for a down payment. Different lenders will have different mortgage options, and although you might not qualify for all of them, there will be some options that you are qualified for.

Make sure you do not get in over your head again. Recovering from declaring bankruptcy once is one thing, but it will not be so easy to recover a second time. Consider buying a smaller house at first, allowing you to save money over time, which will help put you back on solid financial footing.

DEBT-INCOME RATIOS

As we have learned, your debt-to-income ratio plays an extremely important role in a lender's decision of whether to issue you a mortgage, and if so, what amount of that mortgage should be. You can also use your debt-to-income ratio as a quick reference point to determine approximately how much money you will be permitted to borrow. The best way to use the ratio is to figure out a reasonable monthly payment that you will be able to afford based on your ratio, and then use that monthly payment amount to calculate your total loan amount over the lifetime of your mortgage commitment.

There are two main types of debt-to-income ratio that lenders consider when evaluating your credit worthiness. Your housing expense ratio, sometimes referred to as the "front" debt-to-income ratio, is a debt-to-income ratio that measures the total percentage of your income that goes to cover housing expenses, which encompass all portions of your monthly payment, including principal, interest, taxes, and insurance. Let us look at an example:

If you earn a gross monthly income (that is, the total salary you accumulate each month before taxes) of $2,500 and a lender has set a maximum limit on your housing expenses debt-to-income ratio of 25 percent, that means that to qualify for a loan with that particular lender, you must spend no more than $625 on your housing expenses each month ($2,500 x 0.25).

Another debt-to-income ratio considered by lending institutions is your long-term debt ratio. The long-term debt ratio is the debt-to-income ratio that measures the amount of your gross monthly income that goes to all your debt payments combined. This long-term debt ratio includes the aforementioned housing expenses, as well as any other debt payments, such as car loans, credit card debt, or outstanding student loans. As with the housing expenses debt-to-income ratio, mortgage lenders set limits on how high your long-term debt ratio can be. The long-term debt ratio is commonly referred to as the "back" debt-to-income ratio.

The terms "front" and "back" debt-to-income ratio, as they apply to housing expenses and long-term debt ratios, refer to the way the ratios are written in shorthand by lenders. For example, a debt-to-income representation of 30/35 indicates that your housing expenses debt-to-income ratio, the front ratio, is 30, and that your long-term debt ratio, the back ratio, is 35.

You can calculate your own front and back debt-to-income ratios, and your total debt-to-income ratio, in a variety of ways. A helpful worksheet is provided for your use in Section IV of this book. In addition, there are a number of useful debt-to-mortgage ratio calculators available online. Try one of the following tools:

A Debt Calculator. You can do a search for "debt calculator" in Google; however, here is a link to one CNN provides — **http://cgi.money.cnn.com/tools/debtplanner/debtplanner.jsp**

The MSN Money Debt Evaluation Calculator at **http://moneycentral.msn.com/investor/calcs/n_debtratio/main.asp**, or The US News & World Report tool at **www.usnews.com/usnews/biztech/tools/modebtratio.htm**.

When you are calculating your debt-to-income ratio, include all sources of income and all sources of debt, some of which might not be so obvious. For example, your total income calculation should include all sources of incoming money. In addition to your regular salary or wages, include any sporadic income for occasional work; money that you receive regularly through alimony, child support, or a legal settlement package; earnings from dividends; and interest, royalties, and estimates of average income from any commissions, bonuses, or tips.

Your total debt calculation should include all money that regularly goes out, including car payments; payments on any loans for furniture, appliances, and the like; loans from banks, credit unions, or other financial institutions; student loan payments; credit card accounts; continuing payments for past medical treatment; and any other loans or credit accounts.

Whether you are actively searching for a lender, have already secured a mortgage, or are merely considering a potential home purchase in the distant future, it is a good idea to regularly monitor and reevaluate your debt-to-income ratio. The ratio will change as your income changes or as you incur additional debt or pay off some of your existing debt. A major benefit of keeping a close eye on your debt-to-income ratio is that you will be able to discover and avoid the gradual rising of debt and take care of it before it becomes problematic in the view of potential lenders. Staying informed by monitoring your ratio on a regular basis will also help you to make sound, logical decisions regarding taking out loans and buying on credit.

Remember, it is ideal for you to keep your debt-to-income ratio at or below 20 percent; any greater debt and lenders will be wary of issuing you a mortgage or any other kind of loan or line of credit. Anything below that 20 percent benchmark is acceptable, but the lower the better.

Accruing a high debt-to-income ratio can seriously jeopardize your ability to buy a house, and even if you do manage to secure a mortgage, your interest rates will be high and your credit terms restrictive. In addition, a high debt-to-income ratio can be a problem when you need additional credit in an emergency situation. Watching closely how your debt-to-income ratio looks and taking immediate steps to remedy problems and bring the ratio down as far as possible is the best way to ensure you will be trusted by lenders and that you will be able to get the mortgage you need.

INCOME VERIFICATION REQUIREMENTS

Potential mortgage lenders have certain requirements for documents that they will need from you before they will even begin to consider issuing you a mortgage. Among the information you will need to provide to the lender for verification will be documentation that reflects your income, your assets, and your employment.

There are three general types of verification. Let us look at each type individually:

- **Stated verification.** Stated verification requires no direct verification of the borrower's claim, with the information provided speaking for itself and assumed to be complete and accurate. In other words, your word that the information you have provided to the lender is correct is verification enough of the truth of that information. This is the least strict verification category. Lenders often approach stated verification situations by verifying the source of the recorded income, as through a telephone call to your employer, but not necessarily the amount of the income. Stated verification is the approach that is most commonly used by self-employed borrowers, since actual cash flow available to pay off a mortgage loan is generally not reflected in such borrowers' tax returns. Stated verification is also used by borrowers who for some reason cannot meet what is often referred to as the "two-year rule" (see "Full verification" below), perhaps due to a recent job change.

- **Full verification.** With fully verified information, the lender obtains written confirmation from any relevant third party, such as your employer in the case of salary information, or a bank or lending institution in the case of a loan you report. This is the strictest of the verification categories. If full verification is required by a lender, not only must all your income and assets be disclosed and fully verified, but the income so disclosed and verified must have come from a single, consistent source for an extended period of time, often a minimum of two years. In other words, over a two-year period, you must have either been employed by the same employer or, if you are self-employed, must have been in the same business during that time.

- **Alternative verification.** Alternative verification falls between the two extremes. Information that requires alternative verification can typically be proved by evidence provided by you, the borrower, such as your W-2 tax documents and annual tax returns, or by verbal verification from your employer or certified public accountant (CPA). Alternative verification documents are sometimes referred to as "limited doc" or "fast forward" to indicate a modification of the stricter full-verification requirements. As with full verification, alternative verification commonly follows the two-year-minimum rule for income. Alternative verification might not translate to worse terms than full verification in the case of a mortgage, but if you provide alternative verification because that is the best you can do, you might have to meet some other requirement, such as a minimum credit score.

The stronger the documentation you are able to provide, the more creditworthy you will be considered by a potential lender. Conversely, weaker documentation makes you a riskier borrower, which, while it might not mean you will be denied a loan altogether, might affect certain aspects of your loan. For example, you might receive a less desirable type of loan or be required to make a larger down payment. You are almost always better off providing either full or alternative documentation if possible.

There are a few other situations to consider, which might or might not apply to you. First, there exists something called a "no-ratio loan," which is created for people who, for one reason or another, do not want their ability to pay off a mortgage judged by the traditionally used housing expense ratio. Under the no-ratio rule, income is not disclosed to the lender, so how much you make is not used in determining whether you qualify for a home loan. However, in this scenario, the borrower is still required to disclose his or her assets and employment, which are verified. This is to ensure that, even though the actual amount of income is not made known to the lender, the lender at least has the assurance that there is some money available to the borrower to repay a mortgage. No-ratio loans are associated with high interest rates and other potentially high costs and fees because borrowers in a position to require a no-ratio loan are considered a higher risk to the lender.

A no income/no assets verification process (NINA) requires no disclosure of either assets or income; only employment is verified. NINA is particularly attractive to borrowers who are averse to disclosing anything about their finances, whether because of credit problems, sporadic income, or any of a number of other reasons; however, a lender will still expect the borrower to at least have employment of some sort and will verify that this is the case. NINA is similar to the no-ratio process, except that any assets are kept private. Again, NINA loans are associated with higher risk to the lender, resulting in high interest rates and additional costs and/or fees for the borrower.

Finally, the simplest type of verification is no verification. A "no-docs" rule requires no disclosure of income, no disclosure of assets, and no disclosure of employment — no verification of any financial security. This is rarely used and is only offered to borrowers who have extremely good credit, which offsets the risk to the lender of not knowing the details of the borrower's financial situation.

In all the aforementioned approaches to verification for a mortgage loan, there are differences among lenders. For example, under a stated income program, one lender might require a potential borrower in his or her mortgage application to sign a form that authorizes the lender to request from the Internal Revenue Service (IRS) the applicant's tax returns in the event that the borrower defaults on his or her loan, while another might not have such a requirement. In the case of asset verification, some lenders might require a greater monetary value of assets to be verified than other lenders. Find out what a particular lender's specific requirements are in detail before you commit to make sure you can meet all necessary demands and secure your mortgage efficiently.

INFORMATION REQUIRED BY MORTGAGE LENDERS

The following list, while not comprehensive (check with each individual lender for their specific requirements), is a general outline of what data and documentation you should have at a minimum to turn over to a potential lender:

- Information about the property you are interested in and, if available, a copy of a purchase contract

- A full copy of the sales contract associated with the property

- The exact legal address and legal property description (these can be obtained from the clerk of the county court in the county where the property is located)

- Your own current address and telephone number

- Your address (or addresses) for the last several years; a good rule of thumb is seven years

- Your current housing expenses, including your rent or mortgage payments, the type of mortgage you currently have if you own a home, the cost of your property taxes, the cost of your homeowner's or renter's insurance, and the name and contact information of your insurance agent or company

- Evidence of your employment history and proof of any other income

- Recent pay stubs (lenders generally like to see at least your last two if you are paid monthly) and two years' worth of W-2 forms; alternatively, your complete tax returns and any available financial statements if you are self-employed

- A written explanation and any corroborating evidence you might have available regarding any employment gaps or income anomalies

- Records of any dividends or interest you receive; this information can be obtained from your bank, credit union, life insurance provider, or the like

SECTION

4

YOUR PERSONAL
MORTGAGE
ANALYSIS

Once you have collected all the information, you are ready to organize, analyze, and use it. In **Chapter 14,** we help you organize the many pieces of information you have collected. In **Chapter 15,** we provide you with the tools you will need to analyze and choose between lenders and programs that fit your unique financial and personal needs.

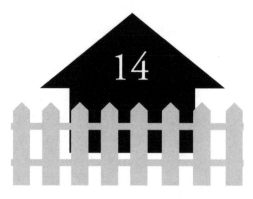

ORGANIZATION OF INFORMATION

Your most important asset when entering the mortgage ring will be your knowledge of your financial situation, the products available, and how to work those options in your favor. Worksheets are invaluable when assessing feasibility, opportunity, and the costs associated with these terms. This chapter includes many of the basic worksheets for calculating and assessing things such as debt ratio, estimated expense associated with mortgages, your home requirements, your estimated budget, and so forth. These worksheets are extremely useful, since most of us tend to underestimate expense and overestimate income, and we often want more than we really need in terms of space.

Once you have this information completed and compiled, set up a mortgage folder with a lenders' comparison sheet so that you can see the different options available.

If there are any terms here that you do not understand, refer to the glossary at the end of the book (Appendix A). Also included in this chapter are many of the terms associated with the mortgage process; please use them for reference no matter where you might be in the process. Many of the terms you encounter will sound familiar, but be sure about the exact definition and whether it applies to your situation.

You should now have a large folder holding a collection of information that includes the items listed at the end of the last chapter. It helps when working on your finances to have worksheets filled out and calculated to see a clear picture of your life as seen in numbers. To that end, there are several worksheets to help you calculate these details.

MONTHLY EXPENSE WORKSHEET

This is a basic listing of what you pay out each month. It is important to understand this figure to understand what size mortgage you can comfortably handle.

Do not underestimate your expenses. If anything, overestimate for those unexpected times of higher costs.

MONTHLY EXPENSE WORKSHEET	
Monthly Expenses	**Monthly Payment (Average)**
Household Expenses	
Rent or Current Mortgage	$
Insurance (house or contents)	$
Home Maintenance	$
Lawn Care	$
Cleaning Supplies	$
Utilities (if paid separately)	$
Water/Sewage (if not paid under Utilities)	$
Telephone/Cell phone	$
Hydro Expenses	$
Gas/Oil Heating Expenses	$
Other	$
Living Expenses	
Food	$
School/Business Lunches	$

MONTHLY EXPENSE WORKSHEET

Monthly Expenses	Monthly Payment (Average)
Clothing	$
Day Care	$
Babysitting Costs	$
Child Support/Alimony	$
Tuition	$
Other	$
Car Costs	
Car Loan	$
Car Insurance	$
Car Maintenance	$
Gas and Oil	$
Car Repairs	$
Parking Permit	$
Other Transportation Costs	$
Other	$
Medical Expenses	
Health Care Premium	$
Doctor	$
Dental	$
Optometrist	$
Prescriptions	$
Debt Payments	$
Other	$
Entertainment Expenses	
Video Rentals/Movies	$
Internet Charges	$
Restaurants/Take-Out Meals	$
Lottery Tickets	$
Hobbies	$
Other	$
Sports Expenses	
Fitness Club Membership	$

MONTHLY EXPENSE WORKSHEET	
Monthly Expenses	**Monthly Payment (Average)**
Golfing Fees	$
Children's Sports Fees	$
Other	$
Miscellaneous Expenses	
Taxes	$
Banking Fees	$
Pet Care Costs	$
Pet Supplies	$
Vacations	$
Spending Cash	$
Other Insurance — Life/Disability/Other	$
Other (specify)	$
Total Monthly Expenses	$

Once you know how much each month costs you, then you need to assess what you have available in cash and equitable assets.

CASH/ASSET WORKSHEET

Write down a complete list of the money you currently have saved up. This reduces your net worth to a simple bottom line. Do not include income — that is listed on the next worksheet.

CASH/ASSET WORKSHEET	
Checking Account(s)	$
Savings Account(s)	$
Cash	$
Stocks, Bonds, and Mutual Funds (if any)	$
Cash Value of Life Insurance Policy	$
Cash Gifts From Parents or Other Relatives	$
Other Assets	$
Total Cash and Assets	$

INCOME WORKSHEET

This worksheet helps to define the amount of income you have coming in each month. It is important to fill out one of these worksheets for each borrower.

INCOME WORKSHEET	Monthly Amount (Average)
Pay (list gross amount before any deductions)	$
Overtime/Part-Time/Seasonal	$
Commissions	$
Bonuses/Tips	$
Dividends	$
Interest Income	$
Business or Investment Earnings	$
Pension/Social Security Benefits	$
Veterans/Administration Benefits	$
Unemployment Compensation	$
Public Assistance	$
Alimony, Child Support, or Separate Maintenance Income	$
Other	$
Total Gross Monthly Income	$
Now take this amount, which represents one month's expenses, and multiply it by 12 to get an estimated annual income.	
Gross Monthly Income x 12 Months = Gross Annual Income	$

This amount helps to define the amount of the loan a lender will offer.

DEBT PAYMENTS WORKSHEET

A lender wants to know what your debts are — listing them as one unit on your expense worksheet is not enough. It helps to understand your credit rating and explain your monthly payments. If your debts are separate from a co-borrower, then fill out a worksheet for each person.

DEBT PAYMENT WORKSHEET #1

Debt Payment	Monthly Amount
Car Payment(s)	$
Other Installment Loan payment With Ten or More Monthly Payments Remaining (furniture, appliances, etc.)	$
Average Monthly Credit Card Payment	$
Student Loan Payment	$
Line of Credit Payment	$
Alimony/Child Support Payment	$
Other	$
Total Monthly Debt Payment	$

Here is a worksheet specifically designed to sort out debts as from a lender's viewpoint. A lender will look at your minimum monthly payment for the monthly amount to be tabulated under monthly expenses.

DEBT PAYMENT WORKSHEET #2

Creditor	Balance	Monthly Amount	Months Remaining
Visa	$	$	
MasterCard	$	$	
Other	$	$	
Total Monthly Debt Payments	$	$	

DEBT-TO-INCOME RATIO WORKSHEET

Monthly Income	Monthly Debt	Debt-to-Income Ratio
Salary/Wages	Credit Card Payments	
Social Security	Student Loans	
Military Pay	Car Payments	
Pension/Retirement	Recreational Vehicle/Boat Payments	
Bank and Investment Interest	Bank/Credit Union/Loan Payments	
Alimony/Child Support	Medical/Dental Bill Payments	

DEBT-TO-INCOME RATIO WORKSHEET

Monthly Income	Monthly Debt	Debt-to-Income Ratio
Rental Income	Computer/Electronic Bill Payments	
Unemployment	Furniture and Appliance Payments	
Food Stamps	Other Credit Loans or Accounts	
Royalties	Other Debt Payments	
Business Income (draw)	Other Debt Payments	
Other		
Total Income	Total Debt	Total Income Divided by Total Debt

PREQUALIFICATION WORKSHEET

Borrower: _____

Co-Borrower: _____

Total Gross Monthly Income: $_____(1)

Total Gross Monthly Income x ____% (housing ratio) $_____(2)

Total Gross Monthly Income x ____% (debt-to-income ratio) $_____(3)

Total Monthly Debt Payments $_____(4)
(list all monthly payment debts that have more than ten months remaining)

Subtract line (4) from line (3) $_____(5)

Maximum Loan Payment Allowed

Enter the amount of whichever is less, line (2) or line (5) $_____(6)

Multiply line (6) by 20 percent for the estimated taxes and insurance: $_____(7)

Subtract line (7) from line (6) to get the maximum principal plus interest payment:
$_____(8)

To work out the maximum loan amount, you need to have a sample interest table. Here is one based on what you would pay monthly based on the interest rate and term per $1,000.

PREQUALIFICATION WORKSHEET

Interest Rate	15-Year Loan	20-Year Loan	30-Year Loan
6.0	8.44	7.16	6.00
6.5	8.71	7.46	6.32
7.0	8.99	7.75	6.65
7.5	9.27	8.06	6.99
8.0	9.56	8.36	7.34
8.5	9.85	8.68	7.69

LENDER QUESTIONNAIRE

Fill out one for each of the lenders that you are seriously considering. So much information is exchanged during these sessions that it is important to take a list of the questions you need to ask and leave with a documented answer.

1) Can you waive any of the costs? If so, which ones? _____
_____
_____

2) Is there a prepayment penalty? What are the terms? _____
_____
_____

3) Can I make extra payments against the principal? _____
_____
_____

4) When can I lock in the interest rate and what will that cost? _____
_____
_____

5) What documents do I need to provide? _____
_____
_____

6) What are the qualifying guidelines of this loan? _____
_____
_____

7) How long before I get an answer on my application? _____
_____

LENDER QUESTIONNAIRE

8) What could be a potential problem with my application? _____

_____

9) Do you represent a mortgage broker, mortgage banker/lender consumer finance company, or a financial institution? _____

10) If working with a mortgage broker, are they licensed by the state? _____

11) As a broker or banker, how much money will you make on this deal? _____

12) Are there any other costs with this loan? _____

13) When would my monthly payments be due? Is there a grace period? _____

14) What is the length of the loan? _____

15) Is there a balloon payment at the end? _____

16) What is the chance that my loan would be sold? _____

17) Am I required to have private mortgage insurance? If so, for how long, and what do I have to do to have it removed? _____

18) Should I purchase owner's title insurance? _____

19) Can I get the closing documents for the loan 24 hours in advance of the closing? __

20) How much is the appraised value of the property? _____

ANALYZE & CHOOSE YOUR MORTGAGE OPTIONS

It can be difficult to choose the best options. To get the best deal, you need to know more than the difference between a fixed rate and an adjustable rate.

It is crucial to know your way through the hybrids of fixed and adjustable interest rates, combination mortgages (with first and second trusts), and reduced or eliminated down payments.

With some mortgage companies offering more than 80 home mortgage options, you need to understand the subtle nuances between them to make an educated decision.

Here is a rundown of how the different mortgages affect the bottom line.

30-YEAR FIXED: THE STANDARD

This loan option offers certainty. It is still the favorite, with 85 percent of all borrowers choosing this traditional option.

Families like the stability and security of knowing what their payments are going to be over a long time.

There is also a 40-year term, but that is less popular. There is only a slight change in the monthly payment over the extra ten years, but the change in interest payments is major.

15-YEAR OPTION

This option builds equity faster. There is a trend toward this type of option. It comes with a higher monthly cost, which can make it difficult for some families and lower-income individuals. The borrowers who can afford this option can save on the overall interest amount and build equity faster. These loans are often a half a percentage point lower than the 30-year option.

For people in their mid-40s and 50s, this is a good option because they will be able to have their mortgage paid out before they hit retirement.

HYBRID OPTION

This type of option lowers initial payments. It is also called a fixed-adjustable mortgage and "7/1" or "5/1" loan. This is because the loan has a fixed rate for seven or five years and then will adjust yearly after this time.

This option is often a good choice for jumbo loans that are more than $300,700. Mortgages of this size exceed the Fannie Mae and Freddie Mac limits.

SECOND LOAN

Taking out a second loan saves insurance. It used to be that borrowers who did not have the 20 percent down payment would have to buy private mortgage insurance to qualify for a traditional mortgage. With the new mortgage options, these buyers have choices.

Some lenders, like Wells Fargo, offer an 80/10/10 option, which means that 80 percent is the loan,; 10 percent is a second mortgage, and the final 10 percent is the down payment that the borrower needs to come up with. A second option by the same company is 85/15/5 (apply the same formula using the different percentages).

If people need to borrow a jumbo mortgage amount (say, $400,000), one option is to make a 10 percent down payment, mortgage $300,000 with a traditional loan, and take out a second mortgage for the difference of $60,000.

Countrywide offers a program of up to $500,000 for borrowers to take out a first loan of 80 percent with a second loan of 20 percent. In this way, the borrower gets to avoid both a down payment and PMI. This option is available to people with average to above-average credit.

If the borrower has excellent credit, he can qualify for the company's Zero-Down-Plus loan. This loan allows the borrower to finance the entire purchase, as well as up to 3 percent of closing costs. The maximum loan amount in this case is $375,000.

SECTION

5

YOUR PERSONAL MORTGAGE JOURNEY

THE HOME MORTGAGE BOOK

In this section, you will begin to understand why bankers, brokers, and lenders do not want you to access insider secrets; the information that is available can save you thousands and cost them just as much. This section covers information crucial to successful completion of the home-ownership process and your opportunity to retain possession of your own money. In **Chapter 16**, we cover the application process and how to furnish the right information. In **Chapter 17**, we introduce you to and then encourage you to involve negotiations as a part of your buying process. This chapter explains why negotiating points, discounts, and lower interest rates can mean thousands to you over the life of your mortgage. **Chapter 18** explores the closing process in detail, as well as the various pieces of the complete mortgage package.

THE APPLICATION PROCESS

Now you are ready for your own personal journey. You have made the decision to look for and buy the house of your dreams. Let us make sure you are ready for the process. Here is a checklist to help you collect everything you are going to need for your mortgage application to make this house yours.

If you are buying this house with a second person, that person must supply the same personal, financial, and employment information for the application.

CHECKLIST	
For the New Property	
Copy of the signed sales agreement	
A recent survey of the land	
Address and description of the property	
Person to contact to gain access to the house	
If this is a house under construction or to be built, plans and specifications	
Personal Information	
Full legal name	

CHECKLIST	
Marital address	
Number of dependents	
Address for every residence you have lived for the past seven years	
A list of current housing expenses	
Your educational background	
Name and address of landlord or current mortgage lender	
Employment History	
Pay stubs for the last two years	
W-2 forms and income tax forms for the last three years	
Employment history for the last two years	
Documented reasons for employment gaps	
Assets	
Listing of all bank accounts	
Bank statements for the last six months	
Proof that the down payment is yours and not a loan from family or friends	
Documented list and total value of stocks, bonds, mutual funds, and other investments	
Documented list of amounts in retirement, like 401(k) plans	
Value of life insurance policies	
Vehicle information, value, and debt still owed	
Documented list and values of other real estate you might own	
Documented list of other assets	
Liabilities	
List of all debts, including loans, credit cards, and any others	
Details of any bankruptcy from the last seven years, if any	
Full explanation of any past credit issues that might apply	

Now that you have collected everything you need, it is time to move onto the next step — closing the mortgage.

NEGOTIATING THE
PERFECT HOUSE

You have your preapproval in hand and have found your perfect house. Now it is time to negotiate. This process can be a bit unnerving if you are new to the negotiation process. It can be a nerve-racking, emotional time for everyone involved. That is because there are so many unknowns, with questions that need answers.

Questions like:

1. Can I close the deal in three weeks instead of two months from now?

2. Should I offer full price in this market? I do not want to pay too much, but I really do not want to lose it.

3. I wonder if I can get that armoire included in the deal?

4. Could I store stuff in the garage a week early?

You have to negotiate for what you want. If you have a trusted realtor, they will be able to negotiate most of the issues for you. Their experience can be valuable in these situations and should give you more confidence in your dealings.

FAIR MARKET PRICE

The first thing is to decide on what is a reasonable market price for the property. Here again, your realtor can help. He can run a Comparable Market Analysis on homes of comparable type, style, and size that sold in the neighborhood in the last year. If the asking price of the house you are interested in is priced properly according to this information, then they are asking a fair and reasonable price. This is especially true if there are several properties in the same market within a relatively small price range.

If there are several other properties in the area that are similar but listed at higher prices, then you probably want to put in an offer within 5 percent of the asking price.

MARKET VALUE

Another factor that affects what you offer is how long the property has been on the market. The longer the property has been on the market, the better the odds that it is overpriced. You will again need the market analysis to understand what a fair price is. You do not want to make a lower offer only to realize later that you still paid too much.

SELLER'S MARKET VERSUS BUYER'S MARKET

The answer to the question as to whether it is a seller's or a buyer's market will also affect the purchase price of the house and your offer price.

If available properties are increasing but sales are decreasing, then you would be in a buyer's market. This can often be emphasized by sellers offering incentives to buy their home. However, if you find that the houses are being sold before you even have a chance to go and look at them, you are in a seller's market.

HOW MUCH DO YOU WANT THIS HOUSE?

Even if you have done all your homework, buying a house is an emotional decision. Sometimes a wrong house is one you feel you cannot live without, leading you to find ways to justify your decision. This may be fine if you take a step back and thoroughly analyze what you can do.

Find several houses that you like. It puts you in a better negotiating position than finding only one house that you have to have.

If you have to have this one house, put in a very strong bid. If not, you are free to put in a lower offer and see what response you get from the seller.

If you want the house and it is priced close to where it should be based on the current market conditions, then you do not want to go more than 10 percent of the asking price unless you have strong reasons. You do not want to upset the seller and lose the house over a difference of a few dollars.

OTHER NEGOTIABLE FACTORS

If you do end up having to offer slightly more than you would like, you might be able to negotiate other factors in that help you out.

Price is definitely the most important factor in negotiating a deal. However, there are many other elements to negotiate as well. Here is where you can get some extra mileage out of the higher price you had not wanted to pay.

CLOSING DATES

Closing dates are important to both parties involved in a house deal. You might need to get into a place at a certain time because your rental lease is up. The owners might be moving and need to complete at a certain time. Each person's date is important and needs to be negotiated. In some cases, the sellers are willing to move on their price to get their closing date. It boils down to the person's needs. If you have to have a certain closing date, you might have to pay a little more to make the deal go through when you need it to.

MISCELLANEOUS EXTRAS

Any item that is permanently affixed or installed, like wall shelves, goes with the house. This is standard procedure. The rest of the items are classified as the seller's personal items. If there happens to be something that you really want them to leave behind as part of the sale, you can have your realtor broach the subject, and if they are agreeable, negotiate for it.

REPAIRS & HOME IMPROVEMENTS

If, when walking through the house, you notice something that needs to be repaired, like a broken window, you might want to negotiate so it is repaired at the seller's cost.

This can be a tricky point. If the house inspection has shown particular problems with the house that are relatively minor, then each party has to decide whether it is worth losing the deal over something minor. The seller could decide to not bother paying for the repair, figuring the house price was low enough that he should not have to. If he loses the sale over the window, chances are, he will be able to sell the house anyway. If you really want the seller to pay for a broken window, you could lose the deal over a few hundred dollars. Again, it comes back to how much you want the house.

This problem is much larger when you are looking at a faulty foundation or roof. That is why inspection issues are so important to protecting yourself.

Each issue that is brought up from an inspection is addressed. It will be either repaired by the seller or waived by the buyer. Often, an amount is assessed and is credited to the buyer at closing.

It is important to have a good, trusted realtor to help you deal with these issues. It helps to have a clear understanding of what you want, need, and can afford to buy, but it also helps to have support in your decision-making. Keep the lines of communication open; discuss with your partner and your realtor all the decisions that need to be made. Rely on the skill of your realtor for negotiating and helping you get your dream house.

CLOSING THE MORTGAGE LOAN

This is the stage of the mortgage process that you have been waiting for, and it can be one of the most nerve-racking.

After you have been approved for the mortgage loan, you will receive a commitment letter from the lender. The final step is the closing of the purchase transaction and mortgage loan.

It is not until this final step has been completed that you get access, legal title transferred, and the loan closed. Understanding what is involved in this process will make this stage go as smoothly and quickly as possible.

At the closing, the seller will execute the deed to your property; the money will be collected from you and disbursed appropriately. The closing agent will complete the documents to give you legal ownership of the property. There are specific procedures, and the requirements will vary according to local and state laws. However, a general description of the closing practices can be helpful.

FROM COMMITMENT TO CLOSING

With firm approval from your lender, you need to confirm the actual closing date. There would have been an estimated closing date specified in the sales contract, but this date needs to be confirmed or changed to a firm date between you, the seller, and the lender.

Make sure that this settlement happens before your loan commitment expires and before any rate-locking agreement expire; this will stop unforeseen problems from occurring. This date also needs to allow enough time for all required documentation to be collected and completed. If repairs from the inspection are being done, then you have to give enough time for that to be completed as well. It helps if you let the real estate agents that are involved in the sale coordinate the closing details. It is usual to have at least three to five days' notice to complete the closing.

Several standard documents and exhibits are commonly required for a loan closing. Some of them are your responsibility; others will be the responsibility of the seller.

The following are included in a loan closing:

Title insurance policy — Every lender requires title insurance. The company that issues the title insurance policy will have researched legal records to make sure that you receive clear ownership to the property. They establish that the seller is the legal owner of the property and that there are no claims or liens against the property. The title company offers both a lender's policy and an owner's policy. You have to pay the lender's policy, and it is advisable to have an owner's policy, too. There is an additional premium you can pay that will protect you for the full value of the property if a fraud, lien, or faulty title is found afterward.

Homeowner's insurance — The lender will insist that you have homeowner's insurance on the property to the minimum amount of the replacement cost of the property. It is important to make sure the policy covers the value of the property and contents in the event they are destroyed by fire or a storm. You have to pay for the policy and have it for the closing. You are not required to select any particular insurance company, but the lender will require that the company meet certain standards and be rated by a recognized insurance rating agency.

Termite inspection and certification — In some parts of the U.S., the property being purchased must be inspected for termites. This will be required for the purchase contract. It could also be called a "wood infestation report." This is required on all FHA and VA loans, as well as for many conventional loans.

Survey or plot plan — A survey of the property might be required by the lender. This survey will show the boundaries of the property, location of any improvements, and any easements, right of ways, or encroachments on the boundaries. Some of these could become serious problems. In some parts of the country, an addendum to the title policy stops the need for a survey.

Water and sewer certificate — You will need local government certification of the private water source and sewer facility if the property is not served by a public utility company. Properties with well and septic water are usually governed by count codes and certain standards.

Flood insurance — If the property is located within a flood plain, the lender will require a flood insurance policy. The policy must remain for the duration of the loan.

Certificate of occupancy or building code compliance letter — If your home is a new build, then you will have to have this document before you can close the loan and move in. The builder will obtain the certificate from the right authority. An inspection might be required to see that it conforms to the local building codes. If there are any violations, they might require repairs or replacements of certain parts. These need to be listed in the purchase contract.

Other documentation — There might be other documentation needed, (e.g., a private-road maintenance agreement if the street fronting the property is not maintained by a municipality).

When you are almost to the actual closing, it is important that you and your realtor make a final inspection of the property to make sure all items are completed in an approved manner.

THE LOAN CLOSING

The actual closing procedure depends on where you are purchasing a home in the U.S. Some states require that you be represented by an attorney; others do not. You might want to have one regardless.

Some lenders use a title or escrow company, some might send instructions and documents to either their attorney or yours, and in some cases lenders might close a loan in their own offices. The closing will be conducted by a closing agent. This person could be an employee of the lender, the title company, or a lawyer that is representing you or the lender. The lender, seller, or representatives might be at the closing. All parties can close this transaction without ever meeting.

The agent doing the closing will have received all instructions from the lender as to how the loan is to be documented and the funds disbursed. The signing agent will make sure you sign all the required papers, and that all the funds are accounted for when the closing is complete.

You will need to bring a certified check to the closing. You will be able to get the exact figure a couple of days before the closing from either the lender or the closing agent. You need to bring the homeowner's insurance policy and proof of payment.

Your main purpose at closing is to review the documents and sign the ones required. The closing agent should explain every document to you, and you and or your lawyer will have a chance to read them over before signing. If you do not understand what the purpose of a document is, ask. Make sure you understand everything.

Settlement statement (HUD-1 Form) — This form is prepared by the closing agent and is required by federal law. It includes all the details of the sale transaction, financing figures, loan fees, real estate taxes, and amounts due to all parties. It is signed by both the buyer and seller.

Anything that is already paid, like the credit report and appraisal fees, will be stated as paid outside the closing (POC). You will be charged interest on the loan from the settlement date to the end of the month, and your first payment will be due on the first day of the month.

Know when all payments are due, as well as any penalties for being late. Chances are good that you will have to pay for mortgage insurance that protects the lender in case you default on your payments. One year's premium can run close to 0.5 percent and up to 0.75 percent of the loan.

On top of the mortgage payment, your lender will want you to pay into an account on a regular basis for real estate taxes and insurance. The lender is permitted to collect the equivalent of two months of the estimated annual taxes and insurance at closing. The taxes for the current year will be pro-rated and you will need to pay for this at closing as well. After closing, you will pay 1/12th of these amounts with each monthly payment. The tax and insurance bills are normally sent to the lender, who then pays them out of the funds collected.

Truth-in-lending statement (TIL) — This is another form required by law. You were given an earlier version shortly after you completed the application. If there have been no changes since then, the lender does not need to provide one at closing. If there have been changes, you will receive a corrected one at closing or earlier.

Mortgage note — A mortgage note is the evidence of your promise to repay the debt. It sets out the amount and terms of the loan. It recites the penalties and the steps the lender is allowed to take if you fail to make your payments.

Deed of trust, or the mortgage — This document gives the lender a claim to your house if you do not live up to the terms of the mortgage note. It details the rights and obligations of both the lender and the buyer. It gives the lender the right to take the property by foreclosure should you default on the loan. This document will be recorded, giving public notice of the lender's claim on the property.

Miscellaneous documents — there will be any number of miscellaneous documents to sign at the closing. Some are required by law and should not be taken lightly; some discuss the penalties for false information; and some give the lender the right to call in your loan, which means the entire loan amount becomes immediately due and payable. When everything is complete, the documents are all signed, and the agent is satisfied that all the instructions for closing have been complied with in full, you become the owner. Now you will be given the keys to the property.

SECTION

6

MISTAKES TO
WATCH OUT FOR

Buying a house is a process wrought with pitfalls and twisted paths. Read on for hints and tips that will help you to safely navigate through these dangers.

COMMON MISTAKES TO AVOID

Purchasing a house is a major decision, and the largest financial decision most people will ever to make. It is important to get it right.

MISTAKES TO WATCH OUT FOR WHEN BUYING A HOUSE

1. Do not look for a house before you understand how you much you can afford. This results in wasted time and energy, and often leads to disappointment.

2. Do not assume someone like FHA is responsible or that you are protected if you buy a house with major defects. The FHA does require a property appraisal and that the home meets "minimum property requirements." However, these are designed to look out for the FHA and not the buyer. The FHA is the mortgage insurer but does not protect the buyer from house defects. The buyer is responsible.

3. Do not skimp on your research. It is the buyer's responsibility to buy the right home at the right price with the right mortgage.

4. Do not buy beyond a comfortable level. This mortgage will lock you into regular monthly payments for years to come. It is important to make sure you can make the payments, cover any maintenance and repair costs, and have a fund for the unknown expenses that inevitably happen.

5. Do not fail to ask questions — many questions. Not all the information you need will be freely offered. It is up to you to ask the right questions.

6. Do not fail to read the fine print. When you decide on a mortgage and a lender, they will send you documents. They are required to do this by law. They are disclosure documents, which will have a good-faith estimate (the expected closing costs when you go to the settlement stage). Read this document closely. Then ask questions about anything that is confusing or unclear. Even better, make an appointment with the lender and go over the papers with them.

7. Do not have high credit card balances going into the mortgage process. Do what you can to lower your credit card balances before going into the application process.

8. Do not attempt rolling debts into new mortgages without trusted financial advice. It is not always as simple as choosing the one program with the lowest interest rates. Sit down and talk to a professional and learn the basics of consolidating your bills.

9. Do not fail to shop around for a reputable lender. The choice you make is as large a decision as the house you purchase. You

have to be able to trust your lender to help you navigate through this stressful process.

10. Do not forget to negotiate any problems found with the house before closing. After closing, it is too late.

11. Do not go to closing unprepared for higher-than-expected closing costs, not to mention the higher-than-expected costs of the whole mortgage, purchasing a house, and moving.

12. Do not ignore your options. Conventional thinking says that fixed rate is always better. This can be true, but not always. Weigh the options, listen to the professionals, and make a sound, educated decision.

13. Do not look for a house without getting preapproval.

14. Do not make agreements without putting them into writing. This includes terms the lender offers, confirmation of your loan being locked in, and any changes to the purchase contract made during the negotiation process. Get it in writing and make copies.

15. Do not delay when supplying requested documentation and information.

16. Do not believe that once the mortgage application is in process, it is safe to be late on an existing debt. It is possible that an investor will do a last-minute audit or check for an updated credit report. Do not give them a reason to reject your application.

17. Do not buy a house without getting it professionally inspected. If the seller agrees to complete any necessary work, have the house inspected when the work is finished to make certain things were done correctly.

18. Do not forget to maintain open communication with your realtor and your lender. Try to avoid any funding delays that can happen. Get loan documents signed several days before the agreed funding date. This will allow everyone to do their final review on time.

19. Do not disregard the significance of your credit report. Having good credit is important to the mortgage process.

20. Do not continuously change jobs. An unsteady employment history will make you appear unstable to a lender, especially if you change jobs during the application process.

FOLDING THE COST OF REFINANCING INTO THE MORTGAGE

Lenders will ordinarily allow you to add in the costs of your refinancing into the loan amount without it being classified out as "cash-out." If the settlement costs come to $3,500 and your loan amount is $100,000, your new loan would be for $103,500. A loan that is for more than this amount would be considered a cash-out.

Your new loan amount cannot exceed 80 percent of the property value or mortgage insurance will kick in.

MISTAKES APPLICANTS MAKE FROM A LENDER'S VIEWPOINT

According to lenders, the following areas require careful attention during the application process.

1. Do not move cash around, if you can help it. During the application process, loan experts have to verify all your income

and assets listed on your application. If you move these assets around, you are creating a paper-trail headache that can glitch your application. Discuss what you might need to move with your loan officer and leave everything where it is until you receive and understand his answer.

2. Do not fail to document large deposits to your account. The loan officer will have to verify the sources of these funds. Be prepared to document all sources of these funds like paychecks, bonus checks, or money from selling an asset.

3. If you are selling something that counts as a large asset, like a car, private collection, antiques, jewelry, or ATVs, you need to document the sale. Keep the bill of sale, a copy of the check you receive, or car title. You might be required to get a certified appraisal. If you do not know what you might need to keep, then contact the loan officer and ask.

4. Gifts need to be documented. It is common for people to receive financial help from their family and friends when they are trying to buy a house. If you have already received this money, then document it; if you are expecting to receive some money, let the loan officer know. A gift letter needs to be signed, stating the money is a gift and not a loan.

5. Keep enough paperwork. Collect and keep everything. This includes bank statements, pay stubs, tax returns, W-2s, 1099s or K-1s, and any other financial papers, like bills of sale, in a safe place. If you have sold a house in the last two years, then you will need to keep your HUD-1 settlement sheet with your other documents ready to produce upon request.

6. Do not set up new lines of credit. The reason for this is simple — it will change your credit report. Once the application process is

started, you do not want to do anything that might change your credit report.

7. Do not pay off credit cards. This is the same idea as the previous point. Paying off credit cards will change your credit report. Talk to the loan officer as to the best way to handle this.

SECTION

7

AFTER THE
PURCHASE

You have bought your first house. Congratulate yourself and be happy.

But do not get lax. It is such a relief to finally have the process over with that people shove all thoughts of mortgages and house buying to the farthest corner of their minds as soon as it is complete. That is fine for a while. But it is important to keep an eye on the financial market and the housing interest.

Now that you have equity in a house, and a mortgage to go with it, there are times when you might need to revisit them. That is what this section is about — the times when you might need to refinance. In **Chapter 20**, we deal with refinancing issues — when is it time, refinancing at renewal time, and when to refinance to reduce your interest rate. In **Chapter 21**, we discuss prepaying your loan. In **Chapter 22**, we examine reverse mortgages. In **Chapter 23**, we examine your options when you run into financial difficulty, and in **Chapter 24**, we look at second mortgages. In **Chapter 25**, we examine the problem of mortgage servicing.

REFINANCING:
THE BASICS

WHEN IS IT TIME TO REFINANCE?

It is time to refinance when doing so will save you money. That statement needs further clarification. You will save money in the long term, but not right away, because there are costs involved in refinancing. These costs could include penalty fees, administration fees, a new property appraisal, and possible title insurance costs.

There are a few clear instances when refinancing is a good idea:

1. When the current interest rate is at least 1 to 1.5 percent below the interest rate you are currently paying on your mortgage.

2. When you are planning to stay another three to five years in the home to maximize the dollar value.

3. When you have time for the process. Complete refinancing can take anywhere from three to six weeks, and that is after you have done all your research and decided on a trusted lender.

4. When you can reduce your monthly payment enough to cover the costs of refinancing.

5. When you are in financial difficulty, like credit cards that are not getting paid off or mortgage payments that are too high to handle.

To tell if refinancing is the right thing to do, figure out whether the amount that you are saving by refinancing is greater than the cost to refinance. That is normally 2 to 6 percent of the loan amount. Find your old mortgage documents, check your interest rate and the term of your mortgage, and see whether you have a prepayment penalty in your contract.

An easy way to calculate whether the figures work in your favor is to use an online refinance calculator, such as the ones at **www.getsmart.com, www.moveinandout.com**, or **www.bankrate.com**.

WHAT ARE THE BENEFITS OF REFINANCING?

Whether you want to reduce monthly loan payments or build equity in your home faster, mortgage refinancing could offer some important financial advantages.

LOWER YOUR MONTHLY LOAN PAYMENTS

The decision to refinance is not based solely on interest rates. A lower mortgage interest rate might lead to a lower monthly payment. However, you can also take advantage of renewal time to extend the term of your mortgage, which can be a good way to save money and reduce bills.

A small difference in the interest rate can save you a substantial amount of money that you can then use to put against your mortgage, reduce your other debts, or take care of long-awaited renovations.

EXTRA CASH AT CLOSING

It is possible at renewal time to refinance more than the mortgage amount, allowing you extra cash. If you decide you need to have an extra $10,000 available, and you are refinancing your mortgage of $100,000, you have the option of refinancing $110,000 and getting $10,000 out in cash. This way you still have only one payment to meet instead of the mortgage and a separate loan payment, and you have the extra funds to do with as you wish.

BUILD UP EQUITY

Refinancing your mortgage to one with a shorter term might lower your total interest costs because you are paying your loan off earlier. Depending on your original interest rate, your payments might not change. However, by refinancing to a shorter term, you can build equity in your home faster.

CONSOLIDATE DEBT

If you have excessive debts that have your finances veering wildly out of control, you can consolidate those debts into your mortgage and refinance the total amount of the debts together into one payment. This is particularly helpful when you are carrying a significant balance at high interest charges with late fees accruing.

SWITCHING FROM A FIXED-RATE MORTGAGE TO AN ADJUSTABLE-RATE ONE

This type of change in mortgage can create short-term savings. This option is good if you are not planning to stay in your house for more than a few years. An ARM might have an initial lower interest rate, but will adjust at regular intervals afterwards. This could save you money with smaller payments, giving you short-term savings. Another advantage is that if your loan has an interest rate cap, you will not have to worry about the interest rate going too high. If the interest rates remain stable, or even decrease, you can save money over the long term as well.

SWITCHING FROM AN ADJUSTABLE-RATE MORTGAGE TO A FIXED-RATE ONE

Having an adjustable interest rate in times of economic uncertainty can be difficult. Switching to a fixed rate allows you to know what the interest rate is going to be long-term. This brings peace of mind.

REFINANCING AT RENEWAL TIME

The refinancing process is similar to the original purchase process, with less to coordinate. There are no closing costs, house inspections, or move-in dates to sort out. You might still have to have a house appraisal done and provide documentation, like pay stubs and account information.

Your current mortgage lender might tell you that it is just not required. Chances are, they will call you in a little early, telling you it is time to sign to renew. They might even be so kind as to suggest that, as you have been a good customer, you can just come in and sign a few papers.

When you first purchased the house and were approved for a mortgage, the lender held the power and you had to conform to be approved. That has all changed.

Now you have the power and they want your business. Take your time. You have options this time around. Make the most of the chance to improve your situation.

Do not be worried that changing lenders is going to cause you all kinds of work. If your mortgage is large and you still have many years left on it to pay, look around — you might be able to save money. That is because the amount you save is directly related to the interest you pay over the life of the loan. The more you save in interest early on in the life of your mortgage, the less you will pay over time.

If, however, you have a small mortgage with only five years left to pay, or if the interest rate savings is less than 1 percent, then chances are the amount you are saving by changing will not be enough to make the move to a new lender worthwhile. Learn about the fees to move your mortgage. If the fees are more than you save, then it is obviously not a good deal to change.

Another consideration, besides saving money through changing lenders, is the other options that are being offered — options that can help you to pay down your mortgage. Can you make lump-sum payments whenever you want, or only on the anniversary date of your mortgage? Paying a little extra each month or even twice a year will have a big impact on your long-term costs.

Make the lenders compete for your business this time. It will save energy and time, and you will usually do better because they know what they have to compete with.

REFINANCING TO REDUCE INTEREST RATES

Sometimes a lender will renew early without you being forced to pay a penalty. In this case, they might give you a blended interest rate. This means that your new mortgage rate will blend the rate you currently have into a new rate. You will not get as good a rate as the current rate, but you will still be paying less overall than staying at your original rate.

This is another time when you need to do your research. This type of refinancing is only good if you still have a long way to go on your mortgage and do not think that the interest rates are going to continue to fall. You do not want to be locked into a longer term at the new blended rate if interest rates are falling.

Talk to the lenders and see what options they offer.

REFINANCING FOR CASH

Some people want or need to have cash and cannot come up with it any other way than refinancing their mortgage, even if their mortgage rate and options are fine.

A good example of this type of situation is when you buy a house planning to renovate it when you can afford to. Then, when it is time to renovate, the way to afford this is often by refinancing. This is particularly true if you have waited a few years and equity has built up in the house.

When you go to a lender, you are asking them to look at the current value of your house against the amount you mortgaged. Most lenders are happy to refinance and give you the difference in cash. Of course, this means your mortgage is going to be larger and your payments could be larger, depending on the new interest rate you are getting and the new term you choose.

However, the cash is yours. This option might be better than applying for a second loan to refinance your renovation. It all comes down to the penalties, fees, and fine print. With that in mind, follow these suggestions for the best deal:

1. Do your research and comparison-shop. Your lender might have an option that sounds good, but until you check out the competition, you will not know how good it is.

2. Let your mortgage lender know you are looking at all options. He will be motivated to find a good solution for both of you.

3. Avoid paying fees to increase your mortgage. You have a good reputation and you are giving them more business. Do not get dinged for being a good customer.

4. Compare what your payments would be with two separate loans — the mortgage and a second loan for home improvement. A typical home improvement loan is for a shorter time and would therefore be eventually paid out versus being part of a long-term mortgage payment.

REFINANCING FOR CREDIT

When you have credit card problems, getting out of it can take an expert. Today, more people than ever are running into high interest rate problems after missing or being late on a credit card payment. Too often, the interest is double what you would expect, and you do not find this out until you end up in this situation. You have to read the fine print.

Unfortunately, credit cards have become a way of life. They are hard to do without anymore, but once a downward slide starts, it quickly becomes an avalanche that is hard to recover from. You need to rein in your spending, get into a debt repayment program, and head toward financial recovery.

It is standard in the United States to refinance your mortgage to clear up your financial problems. Go to an expert for this type of refinancing, preferably a credit expert and not your lender. Getting into this type of situation does not lend itself to fair treatment by lenders. They tend to hit you with higher interest rates, penalties, and other fees, whereas credit specialists can help you to consolidate and possibly refinance so you can have lower payments and still pay off your debt.

Do not ignore these types of problems until you are in danger of losing your home.

PREPAYING YOUR LOAN: ISSUES

Most people think that if you get a chance to pay down your mortgage, you should, but the issue is not that simple.

Before you increase your mortgage payments, there are several factors to consider. These include your current interest rate, the taxes you pay, and your financial situation.

- You need to compare your mortgage rate to the pretax rate you could earn off your money from a different investment to see if that option would make more sense. The lower the rate on your mortgage, the greater the potential to receive a better return through investing.

- Look at the income tax deductions and fully deduct your mortgage interest before you reconsider prepaying your mortgage. By increasing the amount you pay each month, you will be paying less interest overall; therefore, your interest deductions will be reduced.

- Also, consider whether that money could be better used for your other everyday living expenses. You should only use money that is over and above your living costs to pay down your mortgage.

- If you are carrying other large debts at a higher interest rate than your mortgage, you should pay those debts down before paying down your mortgage. Remember, the interest on those debts is not usually tax deductible, whereas your mortgage interest is tax deductible.

- Many people, in their eagerness to pay down their mortgage, keep themselves too tight to survive emergencies. It is important to have a fund set up that will cover any unforeseen problems. Do not become cash-poor. Make sure you have between 3 and 6 months' worth of expenses.

- Instead of paying down your debt, consider refinancing your mortgage. If you manage to get a lower interest rate than what you currently have, you could save a lot of money in interest charges and reduce your monthly payments.

- Another consideration is whether your mortgage has a prepayment penalty. The size of this penalty could cancel out most, if not all, of your potential interest savings when paying off your mortgage early. Look at the time listed on the prepayment penalty. Some ARMs have prepayment penalties for just the first couple of years. Are you still within this period?

- Is your retirement fund in good shape? Have you maxed out your 401(k) and 403(b) accounts? Remember, your contributions are tax deductible. If you are not at the top of your contribution level, maybe you should be looking at increasing this area of your financial portfolio. Your additional mortgage payments are not tax deductible — you are paying principal, not interest. Whereas if you pay an extra $100–$500 per month toward your retirement funds until you reach your maximum contribution, you will do much better.

- Are you planning to move any time soon? The main benefit of prepaying your mortgage is the amount of interest you can save long-term. If you are planning to move within the next few years, there is less value in putting more money toward your mortgage.

- How are you with spare cash? Do you have discipline when you have money available? Will you spend it all or can you save it? If you are going to spend your savings, then maybe you are better off making extra mortgage payments.

- How do you feel about debt? Does it keep you awake at night worrying? Consider the benefit of no longer having to worry about your mortgage by getting it paid down. Peace of mind can supersede other considerations.

- Consider also whether you are paying mortgage insurance. If so, it would make sense to pay extra toward your mortgage until the 20 percent equity mark has been reached.

After considering all your options, realize it does not have to be all or nothing in one direction.

You can both pay down your debt and put money away for investments. Decide how much you want to put toward your investments and put the balance of your spare monthly cash toward your mortgage. Even a small amount of money can make a huge difference. You can take years off the life of your mortgage by changing your payments to biweekly instead of monthly, or by putting any tax refunds you might get toward your mortgage.

REVERSE MORTGAGES

In a regular mortgage, your monthly loan payments make your debts decrease over the term of the loan. Therefore, after your 20- or 30-year term is up, your debt is paid off. The same time that your debt is decreasing, your equity is increasing.

With a reverse mortgage, the opposite scenario happens. A reverse mortgage is a loan against your home that requires no repayment for as long as you live there. In this case, your debt grows larger and larger. That is why these types of loans are also called rising debt, or falling equity loans. As your debt grows, your equity gets smaller.

Most people work hard to eliminate their mortgage so they will have the peace and security of owning their own home. It is hard to change the patterns of a lifetime, and therefore it can feel wrong to look at reversing the process. With reverse mortgages still new and not well understood, it does not help that the most likely borrowers for the reverse mortgage are low-income, single seniors who do not have enough money to live.

It is important to fully understand this type of mortgage before making a decision as to whether it is right for you. Two misconceptions need to be cleared up immediately. You will not be forced out of your home and you will not end up owing more than your house is worth.

A reverse mortgage differs from a traditional mortgage in several other ways as well.

With a traditional loan, your income is checked to decide how large a monthly payment the borrower can afford on a monthly basis. With a reverse mortgage, however, you will not be making monthly payments, so your income is not a concern when determining the amount of the loan.

Another difference between the two types of loans involves your monthly payments. With most home loans, you might lose your home if you cannot make your payments. However, with a reverse mortgage, you do not have any monthly payments to make. You also don't have to worry about losing your home because of missed payments.

A good reverse mortgage should be considered if you need to access the equity in your home. If you have bills to pay, home repairs to take care of, or a retirement income to supplement, this is a viable source of funds.

WHO CAN GET A REVERSE MORTGAGE?

These types of mortgages are not for everyone, and not everyone qualifies for a reverse mortgage. The qualifications are:

1. You must own your own home.

2. The owners are usually more than 62 years old.

3. Your house is your principal residence — meaning you live it for more than six months out of the year.

4. For a Home Equity Conversion Mortgage (HECM) that is federally insured, the property must be a single-family residence, a two- to four-unit building, or an approved condominium or planned unit development. If you are looking at Fannie Mae's

Home Keeper mortgage, the property must be a single-family home, a planned unit development, or a condominium.

5. Your home must be debt-free. If there is a loan against the property, then you have to use a cash advance from the reverse mortgage to clear the debt. If the debt is too large to pay off with the cash advance, you cannot qualify for a reverse mortgage.

HOW MUCH MONEY CAN YOU GET?

There are different programs available. Each program, depending on your age, home, and interest rates, will determine the amount of cash you can receive from your home.

Each is different, and no single program can be said to be the best. Instead, there are differences for each person. There can be up to a $30,000 difference from one program to another.

For the average homeowner, the federally insured Home Equity Conversion Mortgage will provide the best financial opportunity.

There are other factors that determine the amount of cash a homeowner can receive. The amount will depend on the age(s) of the owner(s), the location and value of the home, and the interest rates at the time of the application. In general, the older borrower, the higher-value house, and the lower interest rate will pay out the highest cash values.

The final amount of cash you end up with also depends on how you choose to have it paid out to you.

The money can be paid to you as:

• Immediate cash, paid as a lump sum on the first day of the loan.

- A credit line that allows you cash advances when you need them.

- A monthly cash advance for the number of years you choose, for as long as you live in your home, or, if you use the loan to buy an annuity, for the rest of your life regardless of where you live. It depends on the options you choose.

WHAT DOES THIS MEAN IN TOTAL CASH?

If you take a credit line account, the amount of cash you receive will depend on how much of your credit line you use and whether the credit line is flat or growing. A flat credit line means the amount of remaining credit only changes if you take a cash advance; it then decreases by the amount of the cash advance. Therefore, if you have a credit line of $50,000 and you take out $15,000, you would have $35,000 left for whenever you might need more.

With a growing credit line, your remaining available credit grows at a certain rate. So, if you took $15,000 from the original $50,000, the $40,000 left will grow at a rate of, say, 8 percent a year. This means if you needed more in five years, there would be $51,426 available to spend.

Obviously, a growing credit line gives you more than a flat one. The Home Equity Conversion Mortgage program grows larger each month at the same rate being charged on the loan balance. The Fannie Mae Home Keeper credit line is flat; the available credit never increases.

If you take monthly advances, the total amount of cash depends on how long you actually live in your home and what plan you choose.

If you use a reverse mortgage to buy an annuity, the total cash you receive will depend on how long you live — and it does not matter where you live.

A good way to look at a reverse mortgage is to think back to when you wanted to buy a house. At the time, you had income and wanted to build equity. Now it is the reverse — you have equity and want an income.

So how much will you owe with a reverse mortgage? You will owe the total of all the cash advances you received, including any you used to pay loan fees and costs, plus all the interest. You will never owe more than the value of the home at the time the loan is repaid. Reverse mortgages are classified as nonrecourse loans, meaning that the lender cannot go after anything else you own.

This means that if you live to more than 100 years of age and your home declines in value, with your monthly advances now being greater than your home's value, you can still never owe more than the value of your home.

If you or your heirs sell the home to pay off the loan, the debt is only allowed to equal the net proceeds from the sale.

WHAT IF YOU WANT TO PAY THE LOAN OFF?

If you sell and move, you need to pay the loan back.

If the last surviving borrower dies, the loan must be repaid before the title can be transferred to the borrower's heir. The heirs can sell the home to pay the loan, use their own funds, or take out a new traditional mortgage against the property.

Remember that not all reverse-mortgage borrowers stay in their homes forever. Many people change their minds about where they want to live, and for others, health issues force moves on them. If you are looking at a reverse-mortgage loan, you also need to consider how much equity would be left if you did move.

If you sell your home to move, your lender is paid back the amount they are owed and you will get the difference. If you purchased an annuity, then sold your home, you could receive the monthly advances for the rest of your life.

HOW MUCH DOES IT COST TO GET A REVERSE MORTGAGE?

Each program will have various costs. There are similar fees as with traditional mortgages like interest charges, title search and insurance, inspections, mortgage fees, and origination fees. There is a possibility of other fees, like monthly servicing fees, shared appreciation fees, and maturity fees.

Most of the fees can be financed into the loan. However, the borrower will be required to pay the application fee, which covers the property appraisal and credit check. The property appraisal is to determine the value of the house. The credit check is to determine whether you owe any federally insured loans.

IS IT THE RIGHT DECISION?

You are the only person who can decide whether going for a reverse mortgage is the right decision. That is going to depend on what you would use it for: to increase your monthly income, pay off debt, improve the quality of life, or for cash.

One other consideration is taxes. In general, the IRS does not consider loan advances to be income; annuity advances might be taxable, and interest charged is not deductible until it is paid out at the end of the loan.

WHAT IF YOU CANNOT PAY?

This is not a question anyone wants to consider, but unfortunately, it is happening with much higher frequency.

The first thing to avoid is to deny there is a problem. We rarely do not see what is about to happen. It is possible in the case of a devastating event that we are covered by insurance. These situations can happen to anyone, and there is little we can do to prepare.

There are also situations when homeowners see the problem and do nothing. They wait until they become overwhelmed — usually when it is too late to do anything about it.

The best way to deal with not being able to pay your mortgage depends on the amount of equity you might have in your home.

IF YOU HAVE REASONABLE EQUITY

In this situation, you need to pay attention to your credit. As long as your credit is good, you can always take out a second mortgage or refinance to get a cash-out. The problem is, many people wait until they have missed payments. This drops your credit, and no one will give you a second mortgage at this point.

The problem of how to handle this situation is complicated. It is fortunate if you have a lender who is interested in helping you out. Chances are, however, they will tell you to come back after you have missed your payments. That is because if they have to foreclose on your loan, they are not going to want the equity in your home to be reduced by you taking out more loans against it.

If you wait until you have missed payments, then your credit will be ruined and you will not be able to borrow from anyone.

One short-term solution is to take out a credit line to help you. This only buys you time until you can solve the problem. You now need to recover financially, however, so that you can pay both loans.

FORBEARANCE AGREEMENT OPTION

If you find yourself in the situation where you have defaulted on your loan, it might be possible to get a forbearance agreement written up with your lender. This can only happen when you are in default, and because you are in the wrong, the lender gets to set the terms.

This agreement is a temporary solution and is only reasonable if you think your problems are temporary and you will be doing much better down the road. Under this type of agreement, the lender can suspend or reduce the size of the payment for a set number of months. This is usually for a six-month period, but can be negotiated to twelve months.

When the time is up, a repayment plan starts. Part of the plan is your agreement to make the regular payment plus extra to cover all the payments that were made during the year of reduced payments.

If your financial situation successfully turns around and you can make the new larger payments, you will be brought up-to-date and no one will suffer any loss. The difficulty with this plan is that you have to convince your lender that the problem is temporary. You need to prove your case to the lender.

YOU CAN SELL YOUR HOUSE

You might need to consider selling your house. If you do not see your financial situation improving within a few months to a year, and the line of credit will not be sufficient to get you through, consider a line of credit to keep things afloat while you sell the house. You do not want to be forced into dropping the price to get out faster. By selling your house, you will be able to access the equity in your home.

IF YOU DO NOT HAVE REASONABLE EQUITY

If you do not have a decent amount of equity in your home, you cannot get a line of credit or consolidate debts into a new mortgage.

However, if there is a lack of equity in the home, the home looks unattractive for foreclosure. That is a good thing. The lender will not get his money back if there is no money in the home. Therefore, it is in everyone's best interest to help find a solution to the problem.

This brings us back to a forbearance agreement, as mentioned earlier. Again, if the financial situation is temporary, then an agreement can be drawn up between you and the lender to help you through this time. The problem comes in if the solution does not work.

If your problem is not going to be temporary, other solutions need to be found. This includes loan modification. Loan modification can lower the interest rate, lengthen the term of the loan, change to a different type of loan, or any combination that reduces the payment so it is manageable for the borrower. Any unpaid interest can be added to the total loan balance.

This is a workable situation if the current payment only needs to be reduced to make it doable. In this case, the borrower can live in and keep the house. You are still going to have to convince a lender about your financial situation, but modification is cheaper than foreclosure.

If the situation has no positive change on the horizon, and none of the solutions presented are doable, then the borrower needs to give up their home. There is a chance that if the borrower can find a qualified purchaser to assume their mortgage, the lender will agree. This will save the borrower's credit rating. An agreement like this is called a workout assumption.

Then there is what is called a short sale. This is when the borrower sells the house and pays the money to the lender. The borrower can also hand over the title in a "deed in lieu of foreclosure." Either of these choices is preferable to a foreclosure situation, which will badly affect your credit and ability to purchase another home down the road. These two situations will appear on your credit report but will not have the same damaging effect.

SECOND MORTGAGES, HELOCs

SECOND MORTGAGES

Second mortgages have become a reality for many people. If a family already has a mortgage on their property and they need to fund a large purchase, they will often consider taking out a second mortgage.

It was not long ago that lenders and bankers restricted the amounts and conditions that you could get a second mortgage for. They were looked down upon back then and regarded as a sign that you were not capable of handling your financial obligations. That has changed. There are now many loans to suit the needs of most people, and they have become much easier to get.

When you purchase your first home, your mortgage on that home is the primary lien until you pay the mortgage out. After time, however, with your regular payments, you have built up a certain amount of equity in your home. That equity will help you to get a second mortgage for other necessities.

A second mortgage is simply when you borrow more against this new equity as a second loan instead of refinancing the mortgage. For many people, it is difficult to decide whether they should refinance or apply for a second mortgage.

However, a second mortgage is subordinate while there is still an original mortgage in effect. If the mortgagee defaults, the original lender would receive their money first from the liquidation of the property. If there is any money left over, it goes to pay the second mortgage out. After these debts are discharged, other liens will be paid out.

Since the second mortgage would receive repayments only when the first mortgage has been paid off, the interest rate charged for the second mortgage can be higher and the amount borrowed will be lower than for the first mortgage.

The interest rates are still quite affordable, as there are any number of lenders competing for this relatively new market. In some cases, the interest payable is below the prime lending rate.

People take out second mortgages for a variety of needs, including home improvement, business investments, and raising cash. In today's house-buying market, second mortgages are commonly used to finance a home purchase when there is only a small down payment available.

IMPORTANT FACTS TO UNDERSTAND

- The lender who lent you the original mortgage on the home has precedence over the lender of your second mortgage.

- To get a second mortgage, you have to go through the same basic process that you went through to get your first mortgage.

- You will still have to pay certain fees associated with getting a second mortgage.

- A second mortgage might or might not be more difficult to obtain. This is because with a second mortgage, the lender knows that if you default on your payment, your first lender is paid what they are owed first.

- If you successfully obtain a second mortgage, you will have two sets of payments every month. Can you afford two payments per month?

BENEFITS OF A SECOND MORTGAGE

There are many benefits to taking out a second mortgage as opposed to refinancing. The most important reason is if you have a very low first mortgage rate, but now rates are much higher. It makes sense to get a loan for the lower amount required as a second mortgage at the higher rate than to refinance your whole mortgage at the higher rate. Plus, the fees you pay are based on the amount you are borrowing. Therefore, if you are refinancing your entire mortgage, the fees you pay will be much higher than taking out a much smaller second mortgage. However, each financial situation is unique.

HOW REFINANCING IS DIFFERENT FROM TAKING A SECOND MORTGAGE

There are many differences between second mortgages and refinancing. If you choose to refinance, here are some basics you should be aware of:

- Refinancing your home mortgage means you are getting a completely new mortgage on your home. This means you have to go through the exact same process that you had to go through for your original mortgage to be able to refinance.

- All the same fees associated with the original mortgage costs will have to be paid again.

- Your refinancing rate will be dependent on the current market interest rates and you might end up with a higher rate than what you had before.

- You will have only one mortgage payment each month. The payment amount will, of course, be dependent on the interest rate you get. This means your payment could be lower or higher than your previous mortgage payment.

Take the time to compare the pros and cons of each of these equity-tapping options and choose the one that suits your needs best. If you feel a refinance would fit your needs best, take the time to talk to a trusted advisor for advice.

CHOOSING YOUR SECOND MORTGAGE

When choosing a second mortgage, you can typically choose between three types:

- Traditional second mortgage

- Home equity loan

- Home equity line of credit

A home equity line of credit uses a total dollar figure for the loan amount as the total of the first and the second loan, which is usually 75 to 85 percent of the appraised value of the property. With this type of line of credit, you can withdraw the money any time, you can pay the money back at any time, and you are not locked into a regular monthly payment. Again, take the time to do your research, consider your options, and then decide what is right for you.

SECOND MORTGAGE VERSUS HOME EQUITY LOAN

Many people are confused by these two terms. Let us clarify them.

A second mortgage is any loan that becomes a second lien on the property. This type of mortgage is usually for a fixed amount, paid out in one chunk. As with a first mortgage, a second mortgage might be fixed-rate or adjustable-rate.

When second mortgages appeared in the 1980s, some were structured similarly to a line of credit instead of for a fixed-dollar amount. The person with the line of credit could draw the amount of cash they wanted, when they wanted, up to a certain preapproved amount. These were called home equity loans, or home equity lines of credit (HELOC). They are always adjustable-rate.

It is best to avoid the term "home equity loan" because it is used by different people to mean different things. Some people use it to refer to second mortgages, and others use it to refer to a HELOC. It is best to use the term "HELOC" to refer to any mortgage that runs along the same lines as a line of credit. Therefore, if you own your house and you want a line of credit that is secured as a mortgage, that loan is a HELOC, even if it is a first mortgage. If you want to use the HELOC to refinance your first, the HELOC becomes a first mortgage. Lenders often define a HELOC as a mortgage on a home that is not being used to purchase the home.

HELOC

A HELOC is a loan for a specific amount that the borrower can draw on as they need to. Most HELOCs are second mortgages. However, they are gaining in popularity as a first mortgage.

A lender sets up a loan amount that, instead of being paid out in a lump sum at closing, would be promised to you. You can write a check, use a special credit card, or use other ways when you need the cash.

What is unusual about a HELOC is that it has a draw period, usually between five and ten years, and a repayment period when the full amount must be repaid. During the draw period, the borrower only needs to pay interest. Repayment periods are usually ten to 20 years, which is when the borrowers have to make equal payments to the principal that will repay it completely by the end of the repayment period.

Other HELOCs state that the entire balance must be repaid at the end of the drawing period. This means you will need to refinance again at this time if you cannot pay out the full amount.

With some HELOCs, you can convert them to a fixed-rate loan at the time of the drawing.

HELOC INTEREST

Since you can draw what you need, when you need it, the balance of the remaining funds can change on any given day. The interest on this type of loan is calculated daily instead of monthly.

Monthly interest is calculated by taking the interest — for example, 6 percent on a loan of $100,000 — and dividing it by the 12 months of the year. In this case, .06 divided by 12 equals .005. Now take that amount and multiply it by the loan amount balance on the last day of the preceding month. If the balance is still $100,000, then the interest payment works out to be $500.

To calculate the daily interest of a HELOC with 6 percent on $100,000, take the 6 percent or .06 and divide it by the number of days in a year, (365). This comes to .000164, which you then multiply by the average daily balance during the month. Again, if this is for $100,000, the daily interest works out to $16.44. Now take this amount and multiply it by the number of days in the month you are in. Therefore, for a 30-day month, the interest amount is $493.15. For a 31-day month, it is $505.59.

THE ADVANTAGES

The advantages of HELOCs are:

- Easy availability when you need extra cash to pay off other debts, renovations, medical costs, or even tuition.

- Costs of a HELOC are quite low.

- With some HELOCs, you can convert them into fixed-rate loans at the time of a drawing.

THE RISKS

There are three main risks associated with HELOCs.

1. They are usually structured as interest-only payments for many years, so you are not paying down the principal. To minimize this, try to pay extra whenever you can.

2. HELOC interest rates are adjusted on the first of the month after the FED adjusted the prime rate, so your minimum payment will rise accordingly.

3. You lose equity in your house and might end up with nothing if you sell your property, depending on the size of your mortgage and HELOC, especially when you take into account real estate commission to be paid out.

It is also important to understand that if you take out a HELOC for $100,000 but only use $20,000, if someone checks your credit, your HELOC is counted as $100,000. They do not care if you have only used part of it.

FINDING A HELOC

Researching a HELOC is easier than for a standard mortgage. The *Wall Street Journal* has reported that the interest rate on HELOCs is tied to the prime rate. This is different from standard ARMs, which use a number of different indexes that borrowers have to evaluate.

There is, however, a margin that each lender adds to the prime rate to set the HELOC rate. This margin is different from one financial group to another. You will have to ask each lender what the margin is, as they will not volunteer this information.

The margin can vary depending on credit score, mortgage debt-to-property value, and several other factors. Do not assume anything with the margin. You must ask.

It is also important to find out if there is a minimum draw at closing or a minimum average loan balance. Lenders do not make any money unless the money is used. Find out about extra charges for the HELOC. There are standard fees and charges, but there is also an annual fee and a cancellation fee. Sometimes the annual fee, averaging $50, is waived for the first year. You can also get the cancellation fee waived, depending on how long the account has been open.

Here is a list of items to check. Make sure the figures apply to your particular case and not just HELOCs in general:

- Margin

- Minimum draw

- Required balance

- Introductory rate

- Introductory period

- Lender fees

- Third-party fees

- Annual fee

- Cancellation fee

MORTGAGE SERVICING

SERVICING

The servicing of your mortgage can cause many headaches. Servicing covers the collection of payments, maintaining accurate records of payments, balance, and paying the borrower's taxes and insurance if applicable. Loan servicers are also responsible for going after the borrowers who are not keeping up with their payments and taking the house if the borrowers default.

THE PROBLEM

The problem starts with the fact that a borrower does not select the servicer. During the borrower's research, the focus is on the lender, the loan and trying to complete the closing on time. Servicing does not make it into the equation.

Unfortunately, the mortgage brokers, or the real estate agents for that matter, care about loan servicing. That is because the original lender does not service the loan. Most loans are sold shortly after being completed; rarely does the servicing stay with the seller. The new house buyer has no say in who services their mortgage. They usually will not know who will be servicing their mortgage and will not be able to get a reference about them.

Servicing contracts are bought and sold in an active market. This means a borrower can find out on any given day that their loan has been sold and is now being serviced by a different company. Not only that, but if they do not like the job their new service company is doing, they have no recourse to improve the situation.

The only way to get rid of your servicer is to refinance your loan. However, there is no way to know whether the new loan will be serviced by anyone better. This means that if a servicer does a lousy job, no one can make him do better. Therefore, he is not motivated to improve or provide a decent job.

When we are talking about doing a good or bad job, it is not uncommon for these servicers to be late paying a borrower's taxes or to hold onto a payment to trigger a late charge.

The problem is that the servicing systems meet the needs of the lenders, not the borrowers.

RESOURCES

Excellent Web sites to continue your research:

- **www.mtgprofessor.com/reverse_mortgages.htm** — This informative Web site has tutorials, articles, FAQs, a glossary, and a wide selection of calculators and basic information.

- **www.annualcreditreport.com** — Where you can get your credit report.

- **www.creditdemystified.com** — Here, credit information that is easy to understand is laid out in a simple format.

- **www.DreamsFinanced.com** — This is a real estate search site that features ARM programs, information on second mortgages, home loans, refinancing, debt consolidation, and home equity lines of credit, all for California.

- **www.easierhomeloans.com** — Offers advice on home buying, interest rates, credit reports, the loan application process, and more.

- **www.reverse.org** — From the National Center for Home

Equity Conversion, they offer helpful information on reverse mortgages.

- **www.consumermortgageadvisor.com** — Has advice for home buyers and home sellers, as well as information on residential mortgages.

- **www.compareyourloans.com** — Provides information on mortgages and personal loans and has blogs, videos, and reference guides.

- **www.mortgage-resource-center.com** — Mortgage Resource Center provides mortgage advice for first-time and experienced home buyers.

- **www.GoodFaithEstimate.biz** — This site is a good resource for good-faith estimates; it includes explanations, definitions, and advice on reading a good-faith estimate.

- **www.buyers-assistance.com** — This site offers grants, gifts, and down payment assistance for a mortgage.

- **www.hsh.com** — This site is a publisher of consumer information on mortgage loans; it has current mortgage rates and calculators.

- **www.MortgageFAQ.com** — An excellent reference guide for the home buyer and mortgage seeker.

- **www.mortgage-calculator-low-interest-loan.com** — Offers information about mortgage options, refinancing, and home equity loans in an easy-to-understand way.

- **www.myreversemortgagepro.com/index.html** — Has detailed information on reverse mortgages.

- **www.equalhomefinance.com** — Offers ways to save money and advice on avoiding predatory lenders and dishonest brokers.

- **www.personalhomeloanmortgages.com** — Offers information on home equity loans, mortgages, refinancing, and current mortgage rates; the site includes information on housing trends, market data, and mortgage calculators.

- **www.reverse-mortgage-information.org** — Has a guide with independent information, tools, and resources to help you decide whether a reverse mortgage is right for you; geared toward helping senior homeowners.

- **www.mortgages-magazine.com** — Another site that offers information on home purchases, refinancing, home equity lines of credit, mortgages, and debt consolidation.

- **www.mortgagesaver101.com** — This site provides tools, information on current mortgage news, training, rates, education, and loan calculators.

- **www.nfns.com** — This is a reporting service offering current interest rate information, editorial mortgage, and financial information to newspapers around the world.

- **www.nationalmortgagenews.com** — Offers current reports, trends, and analyses that affect the mortgage industry.

- **http://www.thehistoryof.net/history-of-home-mortgages. html**

- **http://money.howstuffworks.com/mortgage14.htm**

- **http://www.federalreserve.gov/pubs/mortgage_interestonly/ mortgage_interestonly.pdf**

- http://www.performink.com/archives/owningahome/OwningAHomeArchive.html

- www.nw.org

- http://www.alliance.unh.edu/

- http://chicoloan.com/index.html

- http://www.nysscpa.org/

- http://mortgage-x.com/

- http://gofirsthome.com/resourcecenter

- http://www.corp.ca.gov/outreach/resource_pubs/mortwork.pdf

- http://www.fiscalagents.com/index.shtml

- http://www.firsttimehomebuyercenter.net/

GOVERNMENT WEB SITES

- www.va.gov — U.S. Department of Veterans Affairs.

- www.HUD.gov — U.S. Department of Housing and Urban Development.

- www.fanniemae.com/homebuyers/homepath/index.jhtml — Homebuyer information, tools, and resources from Fannie Mae; also has search tools, tips on how to work with a real estate sales professional, mortgage information, and worksheets.

- www.fha.gov — Federal Housing Administration; provides mortgage insurance on loans made by FHA-approved lenders throughout the United States and its territories.

- **www.FreddieMac.com** — Has an excellent "Resource" section for home buyers.

CREDIT COUNSELING SERVICES

- Click Debt Consolidation (**www.click-debt-consolidation. com**) — This site offers professional debt management and debt consolidation services.

- Credit Card Debt Relief, Debt Management, Consumer Credit Counseling & Debt Consolidation Services (**www.debts-relief. net**) — Advice, information, and debt settlement services to help you eliminate credit card debt.

- Repair Credit and Debt Reduction Directory or Resources and Services (**www.freedebtrepair-reduction.com**) — Repair Credit and Debt Reduction is a free directory listing for Web sites that provide quality credit repair and debt reduction services.

- Free Debt, Credit Repair & Bankruptcy Advice (**www.free-debt-advisor.com**) — The Free Debt Advisor Web site is a free information database offering professional advice, tools, articles, and resources to help consumers with debt, credit repair, bankruptcy, and bad credit loans.

- Debt Help (**www.4yourdebthelp.com**) — Help for credit card debt, providing consolidation loans, credit counseling, and bankruptcy advice.

- Identity Theft (**www.badcreditadvisor.com/identity-theft.html**) — Your bad credit problems could be from identity theft; this site teaches you how to check and protect your identity.

BOOKS

- *The Pocket Mortgage Guide: 60 of the Most Important Questions and Answers About Your Home Loan — Plus Interest Amortization Tab*

- *How to Save Thousands of Dollars on Your Home Mortgage, 2nd Edition*

- *The 106 Mortgage Secrets All Homebuyers Must Learn — But Lenders Do Not Tell*

- *Keys to Mortgage Financing and Refinancing (Barron's Business Keys)*

- *All About Mortgages : Insider Tips to Finance Your Home*

- *The Common-Sense Mortgage: How to Cut the Cost of Home Ownership by $50,000 or More*

- *100 Questions Every First-Time Homebuyer Should Ask: With Answers From Top Brokers From Around the Country (100 Questions Every First-Time Homebuyer Asks)*

- *Mortgages 101: Quick Answers to Over 250 Critical Questions About Your Home Loan*

FURTHER SUGGESTED READING

1. *All About Mortgages,* by Julie Garton-Good

2. *Home Buying for Dummies,* by Eric Tyson and Ray Brown

3. *Mortgage for Dummies,* by Eric Tyson and Ray Brown

4. *How to Get the Best Home Loan,* by W. Frazier Bell

5. *The 106 Common Mistakes Homebuyers Make*, by Gary Elred

6. *All About Escrow & Real Estate Closings*, by Sandy Gadow

7. *The Mortgage Handbook*, by William Kent Brunette

8. *Mortgage Loans: Which Is Right for You?*, by James E Bridges

9. *Keys to Mortgage Financing*, by Jack P. Phd Friedman and Jack C., Phd Harris

10. *Buy Your First Home*, by Robert Irwin

PROFESSIONAL MORTGAGE ASSOCIATIONS

Here is a list of professional associations for you to continue your research:

- Mortgage Bankers Association of America (**www.mbaa.org**) — National association of real estate financers.

- National Reverse Mortgage Lenders Association (**www. reversemortgage.org**) — National nonprofit trade association for financial services companies that originate, service, and invest in reverse mortgages in the United State and Canada.

- Illinois Association of Mortgage Brokers (IAMB; **www.iamb. org**) — Online resource for members and consumers looking for information on mortgages.

- Colorado Mortgage Lenders Association (**www.cmla.com**) — Represents companies that participate in the mortgage lending industry within the State of Colorado; includes consumer information and a directory of lenders.

- New York Association of Mortgage Brokers (**www.nyamb. org**) — State affiliate of the National Association of Mortgage Brokers.

- National Association of Mortgage Planners (**www.namp.org**) — Fiduciary-based mortgage services that combine mortgage brokerage, financial planning, and knowledge in federal taxation of real estate.

- International Union for Housing Finance (**www.housingfinance. org**) — Nonprofit trade association dedicated to improving the effectiveness of housing finance professionals and the organizations they lead.

- Connecticut Society of Mortgage Brokers (**www.csmbct.com**) — Directed at both CSMB members and the general public; offers consumer information and a directory of mortgage brokers.

- North Carolina Association of Mortgage Brokers (**www.ncamb. com**)

- Council of International Restaurant Real Estate Brokers (**www. cirb.com**) — Helps restaurants looking for space and developers looking for restaurant tenants in all major metropolitan areas.

- Mississippi Association of Mortgage Brokers (**www.msamb.org**) — Promoting the interests of lenders statewide.

- Merritt Community Capital Corporation (**www.merrittcap. org**) — Nonprofit equity syndicator that pools investments from corporations and provides capital to affordable housing developments.

ONLINE CALCULATORS

- **www.mortgage-calc.com** — Mortgage calculator for home buyers, with amortization, prequalification, and mortgage payment information.

- **www.Calculators4Mortgages.com** — Free mortgage and refinance calculators, as well as amortization tables.

- **www.hsh.com/calc-amort.html** — Generates an amortization schedule, as well as the monthly payment for a mortgage paid either monthly or biweekly.

- **www.bankrate.com/brm/calculators/mortgages.asp** — Calculators for amortization, refinancing information, monthly payments, and more.

- **www.maximumfinancialinc.com** — Offers mortgage loan calculators and current mortgage interest rates for debt consolidation and purchase and refinance home loans.

- **www.mortgagecalculatorplus.com** — Offers a mortgage calculator that figures monthly mortgage payments and creates amortization tables and schedules.

- **www.mortgagecalc.com** — Mortgage calculators for potential home buyers, computing factors such as monthly payments, amortization, down payments, prepayments, and debt consolidation.

- **www.mortgagemath.com** — Collection of online mortgage calculators.

- **www.1mortgageloancalculators.com** — Home loan calculators for amortization payments, interest rates, and buying versus renting.

- **www.hsh.com/calculators.html** — Ways to estimate how much credit you can handle, for mortgages and for other loan types.

- **www.amortization-calc.com** — Estimate monthly loan repayments and total interest.

- **www.smartmoney.com/home/buying/index.cfm?story=mortgage** — Offers graphs of equity and interest.

- **www.mortgage-calculators.org** — Assortment of calculators for new and existing buyers with a loan.

- **www.loanlane.com/mortgage_calc.html** — Point-and-click form.

- **mortgage-loan.amortgagepro.com** — Offers rates, refinancing, home equity mortgage loans, and quotes.

- **www.sss-mortgage.com** — Provides calculators for monthly payments, loan amount qualification, refinance savings, and more.

- **www.jeacle.ie/mortgage** — A mortgage calculator that generates graphs showing your monthly and yearly repayments, amortization, balance, and other figures.

- **www.loan-calculators.com** — Calculators for auto and boat loans, home mortgages, sales tax, calories, pay-off amounts, and more.

BIBLIOGRAPHY

WEB SITES

- www.realtor.org/rmomag.NSF/pages/mortoptionsapr02?Op enDocument

- www.allthingsfrugal.com/fo.prepay.htm

- http://gettingmortgageloans.com/CheckList.html

- www.first-time-home-buyer-center.net/preparing_for_ closing.htm

- http://financialplan.about.com/cs/mortgagesloans/a/ BestMortgage.htm

- www.mortgageguide101.com/

- www.cookco.us/paying_off_mortgage_early.htm

- www.callahanandassociate.com/newsletter/newsletter_ 070808.php

- www.reverse.org/faqs.htm#WhatsaRM

- **www.mortgageloanplace.com/second_mortgage.html**

- **www.answers.com/topic/second-mortgage**

- **www.refirescue.com/second_mortgage.php**

- **www.va-home-loans.com/navigate_va_loan.htm**

BOOKS

The Pocket Mortgage Guide: 60 of the Most Important Questions and Answers About Your Home Loan — Plus Interest Amortization Tab

How to Save Thousands of Dollars on Your Home Mortgage, 2nd Edition

The 106 Mortgage Secrets All Homebuyers Must Learn — But Lenders Do Not Tell

Keys to Mortgage Financing and Refinancing (Barron's Business Keys)

All About Mortgages: Insider Tips to Finance Your Home

The Common-Sense Mortgage: How to Cut the Cost of Home Ownership by $50,000 or More

100 Questions Every First-Time Homebuyer Should Ask: With Answers From Top Brokers From Around the Country (100 Questions Every First-Time Homebuyer Asks)

Mortgages 101: Quick Answers to Over 250 Critical Questions About Your Home Loan

Mortgage Encyclopedia: An Authoritative Guide to Mortgage Programs, Practices, Prices, and Pitfalls

GLOSSARY

401(k)/403(b) An investment plan sponsored by an employer that enables individuals to set aside pretax income for retirement or emergency purposes. 401(k) plans are provided by private corporations; 403(b) plans are provided by nonprofit organizations.

Abstract or Title Search The process of reviewing all transactions that have been recorded publicly in order to determine whether any defects in the title exist that could interfere with a clear property ownership transfer.

Accelerated Depreciation A method of depreciation where the value of a property depreciates faster in the first few years after purchasing it.

Acceleration Clause A clause in a contract that gives the lender the right to demand immediate payment of the balance of the loan if the borrower defaults on the loan.

Adjustable-Rate Mortgage (ARM) A home loan with an interest rate that is adjusted periodically in order to reflect changes in a specific financial resource.

Adviser A broker or investment banker who represents an owner in a transaction and is paid a retainer and/or a performance fee once a financing or sales transaction has closed.

Agreement of Sale A legal document the buyer and seller must approve and sign that details the price and terms in the transaction.

Alternative Mortgage A home loan that does not match the standard terms of a fixed-rate mortgage.

Amortization The usual process of paying a loan's interest and principal via scheduled monthly payments.

Amortization Schedule A chart or table that shows the percentage of each payment that will be applied toward principal and interest over the life of the mortgage and how the loan balance decreases until it reaches zero.

Annual Mortgagor Statement A yearly statement to borrowers that details the remaining principal balance and amounts paid throughout the year for taxes and interest.

Annual Percentage Rate (APR) The interest rate that states the actual cost of borrowing money over the course of a year.

Annuity The regular payments of a fixed sum.

Appraisal The estimate of the value of a property on a particular date given by a professional appraiser, usually presented in a written document.

Appreciation An increase in the home's or property's value.

Appreciation Return The amount gained when the value of the real estate assets increases during the current quarter.

ARM Index A number that is publicly published and used as the basis for interest rate adjustments on an ARM.

Asset A property or item of value owned by an individual or company.

Assumable Mortgage A mortgage that is

capable of being transferred to a different borrower.

Assumption The act of assuming the mortgage of the seller.

Assumption Clause A contractual provision that enables the buyer to take responsibility for the mortgage loan from the seller.

Balloon Loan A type of mortgage in which the monthly payments are not large enough to repay the loan by the end of the term, and the final payment is one large payment of the remaining balance.

Balloon Payment The final huge payment due at the end of a balloon mortgage.

Bankruptcy A legal proceeding where a debtor can obtain relief from payment of certain obligations through restructuring their finances.

Base Loan Amount The amount that forms the basis for the loan payments.

Base Principal Balance The original loan amount once adjustments for subsequent fundings and principal payments have been made without including accrued interest or other unpaid debts.

Beneficiary An employee who is covered by the benefit plan his or her company provides.

Beta The measurement of common

stock price volatility for a company in comparison to the market.

Bid   The price or range an investor is willing to spend on whole loans or securities.

Bill of Sale   A written legal document that transfers the ownership of personal property to another party.

Biweekly Mortgage   A mortgage repayment plan that requires payments every two weeks to help repay the loan over a shorter amount of time.

Blanket Mortgage   A rare type of mortgage that covers more than one of the borrower's properties.

Broker   A person who serves as a go-between for a buyer and seller.

Buydown Mortgage   A style of home loan in which the lender receives a higher payment in order to convince them to reduce the interest rate during the initial years of the mortgage.

Capital Appreciation   The change in a property's or portfolio's market value after it has been adjusted for capital improvements and partial sales.

Carryback Financing   A type of funding in which a seller agrees to hold back a note for a specified portion of the sales price.

Certificate of Deposit   A type of deposit that is held in a bank for a limited time and pays a certain amount of interest to the depositor.

Certificate of Eligibility   A type of document that the Department of Veterans Affairs issues to verify the eligibility of a veteran for a VA loan.

Certificate of Veteran Status   A document veterans or reservists receive if they have served 90 days of continuous active duty (including training time).

Chain of Title   The official record of all transfers of ownership over the history of a piece of property.

Chapter 11   The part of the federal bankruptcy code that deals with reorganizations of businesses.

Chapter 7   The part of the federal bankruptcy code that deals with liquidations of businesses.

Circulation Factor   The interior space that is required for internal office circulation and is not included in the net square footage.

Clear Title   A property title that is free of liens, defects, or other legal encumbrances.

Closing   The final act of procuring a loan and title in which documents are signed between the buyer and seller and/or their respective representation and all money concerned in the contract changes hands.

Closing Costs The expenses that are related to the sale of real estate, including loan, title, and appraisal fees, and are beyond the price of the property itself.

Closing Statement See: Settlement Statement.

Co-Borrower Another individual who is jointly responsible for the loan and is on the title to the property.

Coinvestment The condition that occurs when two or more pension funds or groups of funds are sharing ownership of a real estate investment.

Coinvestment Program A separate account for an insurance company or investment partnership in which two or more pension funds may coinvest their capital in an individual property or a portfolio of properties.

Collateral The property for which a borrower has obtained a loan, thereby assuming the risk of losing the property if the loan is not repaid according to the terms of the loan agreement.

Collateralized Mortgage Obligation (CMO) Debt that is fully based on a pool of mortgages.

Community Property Property that is acquired by a married couple during the course of their marriage and is considered in many states to be owned jointly, unless

certain circumstances are in play.

Compound Interest The amount of interest paid on the principal balance of a mortgage in addition to accrued interest.

Conditional Commitment A lender's agreement to make a loan, providing the borrower meets certain conditions.

Conditional Sale A contract to sell a property that states that the seller will retain the title until all contractual conditions have been fulfilled.

Conduit A strategic alliance between lenders and unaffiliated organizations that acts as a source of funding by regularly purchasing loans, usually with a goal of pooling and securitizing them.

Conforming Loan A type of mortgage that meets the conditions to be purchased by Fannie Mae or Freddie Mac.

Consumer Price Index (CPI) A measurement of inflation, relating to the change in the prices of goods and services that are regularly purchased by a population during a period of time.

Contingency A specific condition that must be met before either party in a contract can be legally bound.

Contract An agreement, either verbal or written, to perform or not to perform a certain thing.

Contract Rent Also known as face

rent. The dollar amount of the rental obligation specified in a lease.

Conventional Loan A long-term loan from a nongovernmental lender that a borrower obtains for the purchase of a home.

Convertible Adjustable-Rate Mortgage A type of mortgage that begins as a traditional ARM but contains a provision to enable the borrower to change to a fixed-rate mortgage during a certain period of time.

Convertible Debt The point in a mortgage at which the lender has the option to convert to a partially or fully owned property within a certain period of time.

Convertible Preferred Stock Preferred stock that can be converted to common stock under certain conditions that have been specified by the issuer.

Conveyance The act of transferring a property title between parties by deed.

Cosigner A second individual or party who also signs a promissory note or loan agreement, thereby taking responsibility for the debt in the event that the primary borrower cannot pay.

Cost-Approach Improvement Value The current expenses for constructing a copy or replacement for an existing structure, but subtracting an estimate of the accrued depreciation.

Cost-Approach Land Value The estimated value of the basic interest in the land, as if it were available for development to its highest and best use.

Cost-of-Sale Percentage An estimate of the expenses of selling an investment that represents brokerage commissions, closing costs, fees, and other necessary sales costs.

Cost of Funds Index (COFI) An index used to determine changes in the interest rates for certain ARMs.

Covenant A written agreement, included in deeds or other legal documents, that defines the requirements for certain acts or use of a property.

Credit An agreement in which a borrower promises to repay the lender at a later date and receives something of value in exchange.

Credit Enhancement The necessary credit support, in addition to mortgage collateral, to achieve the desired credit rating on mortgage-backed securities.

Credit History An individual's record that details his current and past financial obligations and performance.

Credit Life Insurance A type of insurance that pays the balance of a mortgage if the borrower dies.

Credit Rating The degree of creditworthiness a person is assigned based on his credit history and current financial status.

Credit Report A record detailing an individual's credit, employment, and residence history used to determine the individual's creditworthiness.

Credit Repository A company that records and updates credit applicants' financial and credit information from various sources.

Credit Score Sometimes called a credit risk score. The number contained in a consumer's credit report that represents a statistical summary of the information.

Debt Any amount one party owes to another party.

Debt Service The amount of money that is necessary to meet all interest and principal payments during a specific period.

Debt-to-Income Ratio The percentage of a borrower's monthly payment on long-term debts divided by his gross monthly income.

Deed A legal document that conveys property ownership to the buyer.

Deed in Lieu of Foreclosure A situation in which a deed is given to a lender in order to satisfy a mortgage debt and to avoid the foreclosure process.

Deed of Trust A provision that allows a lender to foreclose on a property in the event that the borrower defaults on the loan.

Default The state that occurs when a borrower fails to fulfill a duty or take care of an obligation, such as making monthly mortgage payments.

Deferred Maintenance Account A type of account that a borrower must fund to provide for maintenance of a property.

Delinquency A state that occurs when the borrower fails to make mortgage payments on time, eventually resulting in foreclosure, if severe enough.

Delinquent Mortgage A mortgage in which the borrower is behind on payments.

Deposit Also referred to as earnest money. The funds that the buyer provides when offering to purchase property.

Depreciation A decline in the value of property or an asset, often used as a tax-deductible item.

Disclosure A written statement, presented to a potential buyer, that lists information relevant to a piece of property, whether positive or negative.

Discount Points Fees that a lender charges in order to provide a lower interest rate.

Discount Rate A figure used to translate

present value from future payments or receipts.

Down Payment The variance between the purchase price and the portion that the mortgage lender financed.

Draw A payment from the construction loan proceeds made to contractors, subcontractors, home builders, or suppliers.

Due Diligence The activities of a prospective purchaser or mortgager of real property for the purpose of confirming that the property is as represented by the seller and is not subject to environmental or other problems.

Due on Sale Clause The standard mortgage language that states the loan must still be repaid if the property is resold.

Easement The right given to a nonownership party to use a certain part of the property for specified purposes, such as servicing power lines or cable lines.

Economic Feasibility The viability of a building or project in terms of costs and revenue where the degree of viability is established by extra revenue.

Economic Rent The market rental value of a property at a particular point in time.

Effective Age An estimate of the physical

condition of a building presented by an appraiser.

Effective Date The date on which the sale of securities can commence once a registration statement becomes effective.

Effective Gross Income (EGI) The total property income that rents and other sources generate after subtracting a vacancy factor estimated to be appropriate for the property.

Effective Gross Rent (EGR) The net rent that is generated after adjusting for tenant improvements and other capital costs, lease commissions, and other sales expenses.

Electronic Authentication A way of providing proof that a particular electronic document is genuine, has arrived unaltered, and came from the indicated source.

Encroachment Any improvement or upgrade that illegally intrudes onto another party's property.

Encumbrance Any right or interest in a property that interferes with using it or transferring ownership.

End Loan The result of converting to permanent financing from a construction loan.

Entitlement A benefit of a VA home loan. Often referred to as eligibility.

Environmental Impact Statement Legally required documents that must accompany major project proposals where there will likely be an impact on the surrounding environment.

Equal Credit Opportunity Act (ECOA) A federal law that requires a lender or other creditor to make credit available for applicants regardless of sex, marital status, race, religion, or age.

Equity The value of a property after existing liabilities have been deducted.

Errors and Omissions Insurance A type of policy that insures against the mistakes of a builder or architect.

Escalation Clause The clause in a lease that provides for the rent to be increased to account for increases in the expenses the landlord must pay.

Escrow A valuable item, money, or documents deposited with a third party for delivery upon the fulfillment of a condition.

Escrow Account Also referred to as an impound account. An account established by a mortgage lender or servicing company for the purpose of holding funds for the payment of items, such as homeowner's insurance and property taxes.

Escrow Agent A neutral third party who makes sure that all conditions of a real estate transaction have been met before any funds are transferred or property is recorded.

Escrow Analysis An annual investigation a lender performs to make sure they are collecting the appropriate amount of money for anticipated expenditures.

Escrow Closing The event in which all conditions of a real estate transaction have been met, and the property title is transferred to the buyer.

Escrow Company A neutral company that serves as a third party to ensure that all conditions of a real estate transaction are met.

Escrow Disbursements The dispensing of escrow funds for the payment of real estate taxes, hazard insurance, mortgage insurance, and other property expenses as they are due.

Escrow Payment The funds that are withdrawn by a mortgage servicer from a borrower's escrow account to pay property taxes and insurance.

Estate The total assets, including property, of an individual after he has died.

Estimated Closing Costs An estimation of the expenses relating to the sale of real estate.

Estimated Property Taxes An estimation of the property taxes that must be paid on the property, according to state and county tax rates.

Examination of Title A title company's inspection and report of public records and other documents for the purpose of determining the chain of ownership of a property.

Executed Contract An agreement in which all parties involved have fulfilled their duties.

Executor The individual who is named in a will to administer an estate. Executrix is the feminine form.

Fair Credit Reporting Act (FCRA) The federal legislation that governs the processes credit reporting agencies must follow.

Fair Market Value The highest price that a buyer would be willing to pay, and the lowest a seller would be willing to accept.

Fannie Mae See: Federal National Mortgage Association.

Farmer's Home Administration (FMHA) An agency within the U.S. Department of Agriculture that provides credit to farmers and other rural residents.

Federal Home Loan Mortgage Corporation (FHLMC) Also known as Freddie Mac. The company that buys mortgages from lending institutions, combines them with other loans, and

sells shares to investors.

Federal Housing Administration (FHA) A government agency that provides low-rate mortgages to buyers who are able to make a down payment as low as 3 percent.

Federal National Mortgage Association (FNMA) Also known as Fannie Mae. A congressionally chartered, shareholder-owned company that is the nation's largest supplier of home mortgage funds. The company buys mortgages from lenders and resells them as securities on the secondary mortgage market.

Fee Simple The highest possible interest a person can have in a piece of real estate.

Fee Simple Estate An unconditional, unlimited inheritance estate in which the owner may dispose of or use the property as desired.

Fee Simple Interest The state of owning all the rights in a real estate parcel.

Funds From Operations (FFO) A ratio that is meant to highlight the amount of cash a company's real estate portfolio generates relative to its total operating cash flow.

FHA Loans Mortgages that the Federal Housing Administration (FHA) insures.

FHA Mortgage Insurance A type of insurance that requires a fee to be paid at closing in order to insure the loan with the Federal Housing Administration (FHA).

Fiduciary Any individual who holds authority over a plan's asset management, administration, or disposition, or renders paid investment advice regarding a plan's assets.

Finance Charge The amount of interest to be paid on a loan or credit card balance.

First-Loss Position A security's position that will suffer the first economic loss if the assets below it lose value or are foreclosed on.

First Mortgage The main mortgage on a property.

First Refusal Right/Right of First Refusal A lease clause that gives a tenant the first opportunity to buy a property or to lease additional space in a property at the same price and terms as those contained in an offer from a third party that the owner has expressed a willingness to accept.

Fixed Costs Expenses that remain the same despite the level of sales or production.

Fixed Rate An interest rate that does not change over the life of the loan.

Fixed-Rate Mortgage A loan with an unchanging interest rate over the life of

the loan.

Fixed Time The particular weeks of a year that the owner of a timeshare arrangement can access his or her accommodations.

Flat Fee An amount of money that an adviser or manager receives for managing a portfolio of real estate assets.

For Sale By Owner (FSBO) A method of selling property in which the property owner serves as the selling agent and directly handles the sales process with the buyer or buyer's agent.

Foreclosure The legal process in which a lender takes over ownership of a property once the borrower is in default in a mortgage arrangement.

Forward Commitments Contractual agreements to perform certain financing duties according to any stated conditions.

Four Quadrants of the Real Estate Capital Markets The four market types that consist of Private Equity, Public Equity, Private Debt, and Public Debt.

Freddie Mac See: Federal Home Loan Mortgage Corporation.

Front-End Ratio The measurement a lender uses to compare a borrower's monthly housing expense to gross monthly income.

Full-Service Rent A rental rate that

includes all operating expenses and real estate taxes for the first year.

Fully Amortized ARM An ARM with a monthly payment that is sufficient to amortize the remaining balance at the current interest accrual rate over the amortization term.

Fully Diluted Shares The number of outstanding common stock shares if all convertible securities were converted to common shares.

General Contractor The main person or business that contracts for the construction of an entire building or project, rather than individual duties.

General Partner The member in a partnership who holds the authority to bind the partnership and shares in its profits and losses.

Gift Money a buyer has received from a relative or other source that will not have to be repaid.

Ginnie Mae See: Government National Mortgage Association.

Going-In Capitalization Rate The rate that is computed by dividing the expected net operating income for the first year by the value of the property.

Government Loan A mortgage that is insured or guaranteed by the FHA, the Department of Veterans Affairs (VA), or the Rural Housing Service (RHS).

Government National Mortgage Association (GNMA) Also known as Ginnie Mae. A government-owned corporation under the U.S. Department of Housing and Urban Development (HUD) that performs the same role as Fannie Mae and Freddie Mac in providing funds to lenders for making home loans, but only purchases loans that are backed by the federal government.

Grace Period A defined time period in which a borrower may make a loan payment after its due date without incurring a penalty.

Graduated Lease A lease, usually long-term, in which rent payments vary in accordance with future contingencies.

Graduated-Payment Mortgage A mortgage that requires low payments during the first years of the loan, but eventually requires larger monthly payments over the term of the loan that become fixed later in the term.

Grant To give or transfer an interest in a property by deed or other documented method.

Grantee The party to whom an interest in a property is given.

Grantor The party who is transferring an interest in a property.

Gross Building Area The sum of areas at all floor levels, including the basement, mezzanine, and penthouses included in the principal outside faces of the exterior walls without allowing for architectural setbacks or projections.

Gross Income The total income of a household before taxes or expenses have been subtracted.

Gross Leasable Area The amount of floor space that is designed for tenants' occupancy and exclusive use.

Gross Lease A rental arrangement in which the tenant pays a flat sum for rent, and the landlord must pay all building expenses out of that amount.

Gross Real Estate Asset Value The total market value of the real estate investments under management in a fund or individual accounts, usually including the total value of all equity positions, debt positions, and joint venture ownership positions.

Gross Returns The investment returns generated from operating a property without adjusting for adviser or manager fees.

Growing-Equity Mortgage A fixed-rate mortgage in which payments increase over a specified amount of time with the extra funds being applied to the principal.

Guaranty An agreement in which the guarantor promises to satisfy the debt or obligations of another, if and when the debtor fails to do so.

Hazard Insurance Also known as homeowner's insurance or fire insurance. A policy that provides coverage for damage from forces such as fire and wind.

Highest and Best Use The most reasonable, expected, legal use of a piece of vacant land or improved property that is physically possible, supported appropriately, financially feasible, and that results in the highest value.

High-Rise In a suburban district, any building taller than six stories. In a business district, any building taller than 25 stories.

Holdbacks A portion of a loan funding that is not dispersed until an additional condition is met, such as the completion of construction.

Holding Period The expected length of time, from purchase to sale, that an investor will own a property.

Hold-Over Tenant A tenant who retains possession of the leased premises after the lease has expired.

Home Equity Conversion Mortgage (HECM) Also referred to as a reverse annuity mortgage. A type of mortgage in which the lender makes payments to the owner, thereby enabling older homeowners to convert equity in their homes into cash in the form of monthly payments.

Home Equity Line An open-ended

amount of credit based on the equity a homeowner has accumulated.

Home Equity Loan A type of loan that allows owners to borrow against the equity in their homes up to a limited amount.

Home Inspection A prepurchase examination of the condition a home is in by a certified inspector.

Home Inspector A certified professional who determines the structural soundness and operating systems of a property.

Homeowners' Association (HOA) A group that governs a community, condominium building, or neighborhood and enforces the covenants, conditions, and restrictions set by the developer.

Homeowners' Association Dues The monthly payments that are paid to the homeowners' association for maintenance and communal expenses.

Homeowner's Insurance A policy that includes coverage for all damages that may affect the value of a house as defined in the terms of the insurance policy.

Homeowner's Warranty A type of policy home buyers often purchase to cover repairs, such as heating or air-conditioning, should they stop working within the coverage period.

Homestead The property an owner uses as his primary residence.

Housing Expense Ratio The percentage of gross income that is devoted to housing costs each month.

HUD (Housing and Urban Development) A federal agency that oversees a variety of housing and community development programs, including the FHA.

HUD Median Income The average income for families in a particular area, which is estimated by HUD.

HUD-1 Settlement Statement Also known as the closing statement or settlement sheet. An itemized listing of the funds paid at closing.

HUD-1 Uniform Settlement Statement A closing statement for the buyer and seller that describes all closing costs for a real estate transaction or refinancing.

Index A financial table that lenders use for calculating interest rates on ARMs.

Inflation The rate at which consumer prices increase each year.

Initial Interest Rate The original interest rate on an ARM, which is sometimes subject to a variety of adjustments throughout the mortgage.

Initial Rate Cap The limit specified by some ARMs as the maximum amount the interest rate may increase when the initial interest rate expires.

Initial Rate Duration The date specified by most ARMs at which the initial rate expires.

Inspection Fee The fee that a licensed property inspector charges for determining the current physical condition of the property.

Inspection Report A written report of the property's condition presented by a licensed inspection professional.

Insurance Binder A temporary insurance policy that is implemented while a permanent policy is drawn up or obtained.

Insurance Company Separate Account A real estate investment vehicle only offered by life insurance companies, which enables an ERISA-governed fund to avoid creating unrelated taxable income for certain types of property investments and investment structures.

Insured Mortgage A mortgage that is guaranteed by the FHA or by private mortgage insurance (PMI).

Interest The price that is paid for the use of capital.

Interest Accrual Rate The rate at which a mortgage accrues interest.

Interest-Only Loan A mortgage for which the borrower pays only the interest that accrues on the loan balance each month.

Interest Paid Over Life of Loan The total amount that has been paid to the lender during the time the money was borrowed.

Interest Rate The percentage that is charged for a loan.

Interest Rate Buy-Down Plans A plan in which a seller uses funds from the sale of the home to buy down the interest rate and reduce the buyer's monthly payments.

Interest Rate Cap The highest interest rate charge allowed on the monthly payment of an ARM during an adjustment period.

Interest Rate Ceiling The maximum interest rate a lender can charge for an ARM.

Interest Rate Floor The minimum possible interest rate a lender can charge for an ARM.

Investment-Grade CMBS Commercial mortgage-backed securities that have ratings of AAA, AA, A, or BBB.

Investment Policy A document that formalizes an institution's goals, objectives, and guidelines for asset management, investment advisory contracting, fees, and utilization of consultants and other outside professionals.

Investment Property A piece of real estate that generates some form of income.

Investment Strategy The methods used by a manager in structuring a portfolio and selecting the real estate assets for a fund or an account.

Joint Liability The condition in which responsibility rests with two or more people for fulfilling the terms of a home loan or other financial debt.

Joint Tenancy A form of ownership in which two or more people have equal shares in a piece of property, and rights pass to the surviving owner(s) in the event of death.

Joint Venture An investment business formed by more than one party for the purpose of acquiring or developing and managing property and/or other assets.

Judgment The decision a court of law makes.

Judicial Foreclosure The usual foreclosure proceeding some states use, which is handled in a civil lawsuit.

Jumbo Loan A type of mortgage that exceeds the required limits set by Fannie Mae and Freddie Mac each year.

Junior Mortgage A loan that is a lower priority behind the primary loan.

Just Compensation The amount that is fair to both the owner and the government when property is appropriated for public use through eminent domain.

Late Charge The fee that is imposed by a lender when the borrower has not made a payment when it was due.

Late Payment The payment made to the lender after the due date has passed.

Lead Manager The investment banking firm that has primary responsibility for coordinating the new issuance of securities.

Lease A contract between a property owner and tenant that defines payments and conditions under which the tenant may occupy the real estate for a given period of time.

Lease Commencement Date The date at which the terms of the lease are implemented.

Lease Option A financing option that provides for home buyers to lease a home with an option to buy, with part of the rental payments being applied toward the down payment.

Leasehold The limited right to inhabit a piece of real estate held by a tenant.

Leasehold Interest The right to hold or use property for a specific period of time at a given price without transferring ownership.

Leasehold State A way of holding a property title in which the mortgagor does not actually own the property but has a long-term lease on it.

Lease-Purchase A contract that defines the closing date and solutions for the seller in the event that the buyer defaults.

Legal Description A way of describing and locating a piece of real estate that is recognized by law.

Legal Owner The party who holds the title to the property, although the title may carry no actual rights to the property other than as a lien.

Lender A bank or other financial institution that offers home loans.

Letter of Credit A promise from a bank or other party that the issuer will honor drafts or other requests for payment upon complying with the requirements specified in the letter of credit.

Letter of Intent An initial agreement defining the proposed terms for the end contract.

Leverage The process of increasing the return on an investment by borrowing some of the funds at an interest rate less than the return on the project.

Liabilities A borrower's debts and financial obligations, whether long- or short-term.

Liability Insurance A type of policy that protects owners against negligence, personal injury, or property damage claims.

LIBOR (London InterBank Offered Rate) The interest rate offered on Euro-dollar deposits traded between banks and used to determine changes in interest rate for ARMs.

Lien A claim put by one party on the property of another as collateral for money owed.

Lien Waiver A waiver of a mechanic's lien rights that is sometimes required before the general contractor can receive money under the payment provisions of a construction loan and contract.

Life Cap A limit on the amount an ARM's interest rate can increase during the mortgage term.

Lifecycle The stages of development for a property: predevelopment, development, leasing, operating, and rehabilitation.

Lifetime Payment Cap A limit on the amount that payments can increase or decrease over the life of an ARM.

Lifetime Rate Cap The highest possible interest rate that may be charged, under any circumstances, over the entire life of an ARM.

Line of Credit An amount of credit granted by a financial institution up to a specified amount for a certain period of time to a borrower.

Liquid Asset A type of asset that can be easily converted into cash.

Liquidity The ease with which an individual's or company's assets can be converted to cash without losing their value.

Loan An amount of money that is borrowed and usually repaid with interest.

Loan Application A document that presents a borrower's income, debt, and other obligations to determine credit worthiness, as well as some basic information on the target property.

Loan Application Fee A fee lenders charge to cover expenses relating to reviewing a loan application.

Loan Commitment An agreement by a lender or other financial institution to make or ensure a loan for the specified amount and terms.

Loan Term The time, usually expressed in years, that a lender sets in which a buyer must pay a mortgage.

Loan-to-Value (LTV) The ratio of the amount of the loan compared to the appraised value or sales price.

Long-Term Lease A rental agreement that will last at least three years from initial signing to the date of expiration or renewal.

Low-Documentation Loan A mortgage that requires only a basic verification of income and assets.

Lump-Sum Contract A type of construction contract that requires the general contractor to complete a building project for a fixed cost that is usually established beforehand by competitive bidding.

Maturity Date The date at which the total principal balance of a loan is due.

Merged Credit Report A report that combines information from the three primary credit-reporting agencies: Equifax, Experian, and TransUnion.

Metes and Bounds The surveyed boundary lines of a piece of land described by listing the compass directions (bounds) and distances (metes) of the boundaries.

Modified Annual Percentage Rate (APR) An index of the cost of a loan based on the standard APR but adjusted for the amount of time the borrower expects to hold the loan.

Mortgage An amount of money that is borrowed to purchase a property using that property as collateral.

Mortgage Acceleration Clause A provision enabling a lender to require that the rest of the loan balance is paid in a lump sum under certain circumstances.

Mortgage Banker A financial institution that provides home loans using its own resources, often selling them to investors such as insurance companies or Fannie Mae.

Mortgage Broker An individual who matches prospective borrowers with lenders that the broker is approved to deal with.

Mortgage Insurance Premium (MIP) The amount charged for mortgage insurance, either to a government agency or to a private MI company.

Mortgage Interest Deduction The tax write-off that the IRS allows most homeowners to deduct for annual interest payments made on real estate loans.

Mortgage Life and Disability Insurance A type of term life insurance borrowers often purchase to cover debt that is left when the borrower dies or becomes too disabled to make the mortgage payments.

Mortgagee The financial institution that lends money to the borrower.

Mortgagor The person who requests to borrow money to purchase a property.

National Association of Real Estate Investment Trusts (NAREIT) The national, nonprofit trade organization that represents the real estate investment trust industry.

NCREIF Property Index (NPI) A quarterly and yearly report presenting income and appreciation components.

Negative Amortization An event that occurs when the deferred interest on an ARM is added, and the balance increases instead of decreases.

Net Real Estate Investment Value The total market value of all real estate minus property-level debt.

Net Returns The returns paid to investors minus fees to advisers or managers.

Net Sales Proceeds The income from the sale of an asset, or part of an asset, minus brokerage commissions, closing costs, and market expenses.

No-Cost Loan A loan for which there are no costs associated with the loan that are charged by the lender, but with a slightly higher interest rate.

No-Documentation Loan A type of loan application that requires no income or asset verification, usually granted based on strong credit with a large down payment.

Nonassumption Clause A provision in a loan agreement that prohibits transferring a mortgage to another borrower without approval from the lender.

Nondiscretionary Funds The funds that are allocated to an investment manager who must have approval from the investor for each transaction.

One-Year Adjustable-Rate Mortgage An ARM for which the interest rate changes annually, generally based on movements of a published index plus a specified margin.

Open-End Fund A type of commingled fund with an infinite life, always accepting new investor capital and making new investments in property.

Option A condition in which the buyer pays for the right to purchase a property within a certain period of time without the obligation to buy.

Option ARM Loan A type of mortgage in which the borrower has a variety of payment options each month.

Original Principal Balance The total principal owed on a mortgage before a borrower has made a payment.

Owner Financing A transaction in which the property seller agrees to finance all or part of the amount of the purchase.

Partial Payment An amount paid that is not large enough to cover the normal monthly payment on a mortgage loan.

Partial Sales The act of selling a real estate interest that is smaller than the whole property.

Payment Cap The maximum amount a monthly payment may increase on an ARM.

Payment Change Date The date on which a new payment amount takes effect on an ARM or GPM, usually in the month directly after the adjustment date.

Pension Liability The full amount of capital that is required to finance vested pension fund benefits.

Per-Diem Interest The interest that is charged or accrued daily.

Periodic Payment Cap The highest amount that payments can increase or decrease during a given adjustment period on an ARM.

Periodic Rate Cap The maximum amount that the interest rate can increase or decrease during a given adjustment period on an ARM.

Permanent Loan A long-term property mortgage.

Preapproval The complete analysis a lender makes regarding a potential borrower's ability to pay for a home, as well as a confirmation of the proposed amount to be borrowed.

Prepayment Penalty A penalty that may be charged to the borrower when he pays off a loan before the planned maturity date.

Prime Rate The best interest rate

reserved for a bank's preferred customers.

Principal The amount of money originally borrowed in a mortgage, before interest is included and with any payments subtracted.

Principal Payments The lender's return of invested capital.

Private Debt Mortgages or other liabilities for which an individual is responsible.

Private Equity A real estate investment that has been acquired by a noncommercial entity.

Private Mortgage Insurance (PMI) A type of policy that a lender requires when the borrower's down payment or home equity percentage is under 20 percent of the value of the property.

Purchase-Money Mortgage (PMM) A mortgage obtained by a borrower that serves as partial payment for a property.

Qualified Plan Any employee benefit plan that the IRS has approved as a tax-exempt plan.

Qualifying Ratio The measurement a lender uses to determine how much they are willing to lend to a potential buyer.

Rate-Improvement Mortgage A loan that includes a clause that entitles a borrower to a one-time-only cut in the interest rate without having to refinance.

Real Estate Agent An individual who is licensed to negotiate and transact the real estate sales.

Real Estate Fundamentals The factors that drive the value of property.

Realtor A real estate agent or broker who is an active member of a local real estate board affiliated with the National Association of Realtors.

Recorder A public official who records transactions that affect real estate in the area.

Recording The documentation that the registrar's office keeps of the details of properly executed legal documents.

Recording Fee A fee real estate agents charge for moving the sale of a piece of property into the public record.

Recourse The option a lender has for recovering losses against the personal assets of a secondary party who is also liable for a debt that is in default.

Refinance Transaction The act of paying off an existing loan using the funding gained from a new loan that uses the same property as security.

Regulation Z A federal legislation under the Truth in Lending Act that requires lenders to advise the borrower in writing of all costs that are associated with the credit portion of a financial transaction.

Rehabilitation Mortgage A loan meant to fund the repairing and improving of a resale home or building.

REIT (Real Estate Investment Trust) A trust corporation that combines the capital of several investors for the purpose of acquiring or providing funding for real estate.

Remaining Balance The amount of the principal on a home loan that has not yet been paid.

Remaining Term The original term of the loan after the number of payments made has been subtracted.

REMIC (Real Estate Mortgage Investment Conduit) An investment vehicle that is designed to hold a pool of mortgages solely to issue multiple classes of mortgage-backed securities in a way that avoids doubled corporate tax.

Renewal Option A clause in a lease agreement that allows a tenant to extend the term of a lease.

Repayment Plan An agreement made to repay late installments or advances.

Revolving Debt A credit arrangement that enables a customer to borrow against a predetermined line of credit when purchasing goods and services.

Sale-Leaseback An arrangement in which a seller deeds a property, or part of it, to a buyer in exchange for money or the equivalent, then leases the property from the new owner.

Sales Contract An agreement that both the buyer and seller sign defining the terms of a property sale.

Secured Loan A loan that is secured by some sort of collateral.

Security Deposit An amount of money a tenant gives to a landlord to secure the performance of terms in a lease agreement.

Seller Financing A type of funding in which the borrower may use part of the equity in the property to finance the purchase.

Settlement or Closing Fees Fees that the escrow agent receives for carrying out the written instructions in the agreement between borrower and lender and/or buyer and seller.

Survey A document or analysis containing the precise measurements of a piece of property as performed by a licensed surveyor.

Tax Lien A type of lien placed against a property if the owner has not paid property or personal taxes.

Title The legal written document that provides someone ownership in a piece of real estate.

Total Acres The complete amount of

land area that is contained within a real estate investment.

Total Assets The final amount of all gross investments, cash and equivalents, receivables, and other assets as they are presented on the balance sheet.

Total Commitment The complete funding amount that is promised once all specified conditions have been met.

Total Expense Ratio The comparison of monthly debt obligations to gross monthly income.

Total Loan Amount The basic amount of the loan plus any additional financed closing costs.

Total Principal Balance The sum of all debt, including the original loan amount adjusted for subsequent payments and any unpaid items that may be included in the principal balance by the mortgage note or by law.

Transfer of Ownership Any process in which a property changes hands from one owner to another.

Transfer Tax An amount specified by state or local authorities when ownership in a piece of property changes hands.

Triple Net Lease A lease that requires the tenant to pay all property expenses on top of the rental payments.

Two-Step Mortgage An ARM with two

different interest rates: one for the loan's first five or seven years and another for the remainder of the loan term.

Unrecorded Deed A deed that transfers right of ownership from one owner to another without being officially documented.

VA Loan A mortgage through the VA program in which a down payment is not necessarily required.

Variable Rate Also called adjustable rate. The interest rate on a loan that varies over the term of the loan according to a predetermined index.

Variable Rate Mortgage (VRM) A loan in which the interest rate changes according to fluctuations in particular indexes.

Veterans Affairs (VA) A federal government agency that assists veterans in purchasing a home without a down payment.

Waiting Period The period of time between initially filing a registration statement and the date it becomes effective.

Wraparound Mortgage A loan obtained by a buyer to use for the remaining balance on the seller's first mortgage, as well as an additional amount requested by the seller.

AUTHOR DEDICATION

———

A book is not pulled together in one day and a writing career is not established overnight. Along the way, there are many bumps and turns that can stall or stop the process. It is during these times that you realize who your supporters are, and who believes in you and what you are trying to accomplish. My life is no different, except that maybe I have been more blessed than most. I have several good friends that do not judge or criticize me. They love me. They honor me and the path that I have chosen. Then there is my family. It is easy to say they support me because that is what families do, but I would like to think their support is based on their belief in me. My four children have always been my strongest supporters, firmly believing in their mother's ability to 'make it big.' Without these special people in my life, that long and twisted road would have been very lonely. Thank you to all those that walked by my side.

AUTHOR BIOGRAPHY

Dale Mayer

Dale Mayer is a certified technical writer, editor, and researcher with a passion for the written word. For over a decade, she has honored that passion both at work and at home. Besides her very busy freelance business, she is also an avid fiction writer. At this time, she has completed five novels; her sixth is in progress. She also has five completed screenplays to her credit. She enjoys writing non-fiction, because it forces her brain out of the clouds and back to the world in which we all live in. Researching, writing, and then organizing all the parts and pieces together into a coherent and easy to read package is just plain fun! She can be contacted through her Web site, **www.dalemayer.com**.

INDEX

YOUR REAL ESTATE CLOSING EXPLAINED SIMPLY: WHAT SMART BUYERS & SELLERS NEED TO KNOW

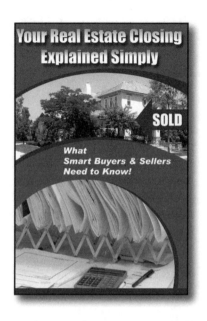

This book is a complete explanation of the real estate closing process and escrow. (Escrow is a neutral third party that follows the instructions from buyer and seller of the property. It makes sure that the required funds are in the escrow account before the deed to the home is recorded in the buyer's name.) Easy-to-understand, it will help you save time, money, and guide you around pitfalls. Subjects covered are the mortgages, your closing agent, tittle commitment, survey, deed, bill of sale, affidavit of title, leases, assignment of contracts, right of first refusal, assessments, closing statement, power of attorney, personal information affidavit, joint tenancy affidavit, inspections, attorney approval contingency, lead paint disclosure, and much more. The book includes numerous forms and easy-to-use checklists as well as information particular to each state..

ISBN-10: 1-60138-032-1 • ISBN-13: 978-1-60138-032-6
288 Pages • $24.95

To order call 1-800-814-1132 or visit www.atlantic-pub.com

301 Simple Things
You Can Do To sell Your Home Now and For More Money Than You Thought: How to Inexpensively Reorganize, Stage, and Prepare your Home for Sale

You may not be able to improve the market value of your house, but you can improve its marketability. In this book you will learn how small color changes will increase your home's value, minor repairs and de-cluttering tricks, how to rearrange your furniture, how to look at your house from the buyer's viewpoint, which minor changes will bring you the greatest return, how to bring out a home's best features, how to minimize problem areas, how to position your house for the marketplace, how to use design psychology techniques, lighting techniques, landscaping secrets, how to ensure a positive traffic flow through rooms, and much more.

ISBN-10: 0-910627-06-1 • ISBN-13: 978-0-910627-06-1
288 Pages • $24.95

To order call 1-800-814-1132 or visit www.atlantic-pub.com

MAR 3 2008 CHRISTIANSBURG LIBRARY
MONTGOMERY-FLOYD REGIONAL LIBRARY SYSTEM

DID YOU BORROW THIS COPY?

Have you been borrowing a copy of *The Home Mortgage Book: Insider Information Your Banker & Broker Don't Want You to Know* from a friend, colleague, or library? Wouldn't you like your own copy for quick and easy reference? To order, photocopy the form below and send to:

Atlantic Publishing Company
1405 SW 6th Ave • Ocala, FL 34471-0640

Withdrawn From Montgomery-Floyd Regional Library

YES!

Send me_____copy(ies) of *The Home Mortgage Book: Insider Information Your Banker & Broker Don't Want You to Know* (ISBN: 978-0-910627-84-9) for $21.95 plus $7.00 for shipping and handling.

Please Print

_____
Name

_____
Organization Name

_____
Address

_____
City, State, Zip

❏ My check or money order is enclosed. *Please make checks payable to Atlantic Publishing Company.*

❏ My purchase order is attached. *PO #* _____

www.atlantic-pub.com • e-mail: sales@atlantic-pub.com

Order toll-free 800-814-1132

FAX 352-622-1875

Atlantic Publishing Company
1405 SW 6th Ave • Ocala, FL 34471-0640

Add $7.00 for USPS shipping and handling. For Florida residents PLEASE add the appropriate sales tax for your county.